There is little, if any, place for sufferi̇... American Christians. Yet everywhere a̲ro̲u̲n̲d̲ ... *We are suffering. This Too Shall Last* examines—with moving honesty, sharp insight, and deep faith—what it means to suffer, how to suffer, and why an understanding and acceptance of suffering is essential to Christian belief and the Christian life.

—KAREN SWALLOW PRIOR, author, *On Reading Well: Finding the Good Life through Great Books*

In this remarkable debut, K.J. Ramsey arrives as both neighbor and guide, deftly weaving vulnerable storytelling, clear theology, and a compelling therapeutic framework. Against a backdrop of suffering, K.J. awakens us to our tender, tear-streaked Savior, who holds our hand through it all. Refreshing and luminous, this book has the power to reshape our faith and fortify our communities.

—SHANNAN MARTIN, author, *The Ministry of Ordinary Places* and *Falling Free*

In a world where dark nights of the soul are inescapable, we need help seeing that it is not our circumstances that reveal to us the truth about God, but the truth of God that reveals to us the meaning in our circumstances. As Paul said of his own thorn in the flesh, it is in our weakness that the power of God is most at work, transforming our thorns into crowns. Loved and kept by a strong, steady God who works all things together for good, hope and meaning wait for us in the shadows. K.J. does a very good job opening our eyes to this reality.

—SCOTT SAULS, pastor, Christ Presbyterian Church; author, *A Gentle Answer*

The truest words in this book are "this book is not a before and after story." K.J. looks without caveat into the reality of suffering, her own and others, and doesn't flinch from the truths to be mined there. Neither does she paint a picture of suffering as glorious or easy. She tells the truth, the gritty, mired truth about suffering, and instead of merely offering a path forward, she stands beside her reader for the journey.

—LORE FERGUSON WILBERT, author, *Handle with Care: How Jesus Redeems the Power of Touch in Life and Ministry*

When I first saw the cover of this book and read the title, I knew I needed to get my hands on it. Turns out, you really can judge a book by its cover. For anyone who is hurting, for anyone whose life isn't turning out like they had hoped, this is an extraordinary invitation, from a credible voice, to be held by God in the middle of suffering. Don't miss this book.

—JENNIFER DUKES LEE, author, *It's All under Control*

K.J.'s exquisite offering comes from the depths of suffering and from a whole heart. She's a woman whose vulnerability makes it easy for you to relax into the wild and wondrous story of God, and to see how God's design of human brains and bodies invites participation in the life of the suffering servant. A wondrously healing book.

—CHUCK DEGROAT, writer; therapist; Professor of Pastoral Care and Christian Spirituality, Western Theological Seminary

In a market so often dominated by easy answers and spiritual platitudes, K.J. has crafted a work of masterful complexity and depth. She seamlessly weaves pieces of memoir with universally applicable truths, tearfully soaked in a wisdom birthed from her intimate understanding of pain. With prose that often feels more like poetry than instruction, K.J. empathetically guides readers through a nuanced reflection on suffering, faith, community, and embodiment. In the end, we're left in the perfect tension between comforted and challenged, with a newfound ability to see the beauty in that sacred dissonance.

—STEPHANIE TAIT, author, *The View from Rock Bottom: Discovering God's Embrace in Our Pain*

Of all people, those who follow Jesus should have a framework to relate to suffering and loss. However, we often find ourselves lacking the internal and external resources to navigate the harsh realities of life. K.J. offers us a powerful way forward to help us find God in the midst of suffering that has no end date in sight. I highly recommend it!

—RICH VILLODAS, lead pastor, New Life Fellowship

What do you do when your trial isn't merely a matter of making it through to the other side? You're not going to get better or your situation will never get resolved. And how do you reconcile such things with your faith and those seemingly unanswered prayers? I am so grateful for the deep and compassionate treatment of these challenging questions in this new book. K.J. is a beautiful writer with a strong and thoughtful response to the heartache of suffering. You will find no pat answers here, but I daresay you will find unexpected hope.

—LISA JACOBSON, Club31Women.com

The kingdom of God is both "now" and "not yet," but what are we supposed to do when it seems like it's mostly "not yet"? Drawing on her experiences of God's grace in the midst of chronic suffering, K.J. delivers penetrating insights about the present age that most of us never see but that we all so desperately need. There is better news than the American Dream, and this is it.

—BRIAN FIKKERT, coauthor, *When Helping Hurts* and *Becoming Whole: Why the Opposite of Poverty Isn't the American Dream*

I opened the pages of this book and found grace. You won't find pat answers or quick fixes here. Instead, you'll find the healing balm of honesty, vulnerability, and shared experience. K.J. Ramsey is a gift.

—ALISON COOK, therapist; author, *Boundaries for Your Soul*

This book is not for everyone: it's for the weary. K.J. is a modern-day prophet. The job of a prophet is to speak truths, particularly those truths that expose the illusions of the dominant culture. In this book, K.J. exposes illusions that bind us, but she doesn't stop there. Her goal is to invite you into your story. Your story matters more than you think, particularly your story of suffering. Why? Because, as K.J. unfolds in the following pages, it is in your story of suffering that you mysteriously come to know the One who gets down on the floor with you, and sits in the fire of your ache. All you who are weary, welcome.

—ADAM YOUNG, therapist; host, *The Place We Find Ourselves* podcast

K.J. works from her own turbulent experience to weave empathy, therapeutic wisdom, and rich theology into an artful gift. All who suffer will find deep-running currents of grace in her work. Rarely do I find such a work that models so powerfully the therapeutic properties of good theology, from the Trinity to ecclesiology.

—DON J. PAYNE, Associate Professor of Theology, Denver Seminary

A must-read for patients and anyone with constant pain or suffering. K.J. will change your relationship with pain forever as she shares her journey, knowledge, spirituality, and strategies to find peace and grace during lasting suffering.

—JOSE NATIVI-NICOLAU, transplant cardiologist

I serve a church that recently lost its beloved founding pastor to brain cancer. What do we do when it is life that withers and suffering that blossoms? When pain simply doesn't pass? K.J.'s words pulse with gospel truth and grace for those who live in the middle of a still-painful storyline.

—JORDAN KOLOGE, rector/pastor, Church of the Advent

Just when I needed it most, this book was given to me. Within these pages I found language for all that I've felt and hope for all that I need. Through her vulnerability and beautiful writing, K.J. shows us how we can find grace in suffering that lingers and strength in God's presence that lasts. The invitation your heart longs for in the middle of your brokenness is waiting for you here.

—RENEE SWOPE, author, *A Confident Heart*; former executive director and radio cohost, Proverbs 31 Ministries

K.J. is real in the deepest and best sense of the word. Her suffering is tragically real. But more important, her God—revealed in Jesus and in her pain—is real. Instead of an escape from suffering, this book gracefully, eloquently, and truthfully invites us into real life with Jesus in the midst of real suffering.

—HOWARD BAKER, Assistant Professor of Christian Formation, Denver Seminary

In this compelling book, K.J. brings together the keen insight of a therapist, the poignant testimony of a person suffering from chronic illness, and the resounding hope of a follower of Jesus. Theologically articulate and bracingly honest, K.J. points the church to its deepest identity as children of the wondrous triune God. I am grateful for this book!

—J. TODD BILLINGS, Girod Professor of Reformed Theology, Western Theological Seminary

Absorb K.J.'s book. Spend the time you need to integrate her words into the fabric of your soul. There is a simple reason to make such an investment. This book is a powerful and accessible integration of theology (e.g union with Christ) and neurology (e.g. attachment patterns) in service to the relational modality that makes suffering sufferable. K.J. makes it clear how and why suffering is redeemed through honesty and vulnerability with someone who loves you enough to listen well.

—JAMES E. COFIELD, coauthor, *The Relational Soul*

THIS
TOO
SHALL
LAST

THIS TOO SHALL LAST

FINDING GRACE WHEN
SUFFERING LINGERS

K.J. RAMSEY

ZONDERVAN
REFLECTIVE

ZONDERVAN REFLECTIVE

This Too Shall Last
Copyright © 2020 by Katie Jo Ramsey

Requests for information should be addressed to:
Zondervan, *3900 Sparks Dr. SE, Grand Rapids, Michigan 49546*

ISBN 978-0-310-10725-5 (softcover)

ISBN 978-0-310-10727-9 (audio)

ISBN 978-0-310-10726-2 (ebook)

Published in association with the literary agency of Wolgemuth and Associates, Inc.

Cover design: Christopher Tobias / Tobias Design
Cover photo: © Sandra_M / Shutterstock
Interior design: Denise Froehlich

Printed in the United States of America

20 21 22 23 24 25 /LSC/ 10 9 8 7 6 5 4 3 2 1

For Ryan,
who sows in tears with me.
Your love is grace.

Those who sow in tears
will reap with shouts of joy.

—PSALM 126:5

CONTENTS

CONTENTS

FOREWORD

Where is God to be found when everything hurts and the words that others intend as encouragement fall flat like dead cliches? It may surprise some people that I believe the hardest theological question is captured by three simple words: is God good? Whether we confront injustice, troubled relationships, or physical pain, the same question can taunt each of us: is God good? We wonder where he is and what he thinks about our suffering. Does he know? Does he care? Why is he so quiet?

For most of us, the best help with such questions may be found not so much in philosophical arguments as in real life stories. Stories matter. Experience matters. Our hurts and hopes matter. But what we believe also greatly matters, so how are we to make sense of life when we find ourselves in the midst of such troubles and confusion? We need a witness.

"There is no way to Christ without martyrs, without witnesses,"[1] concludes historian Robert Louis Wilken, writing about the first centuries of the church. *Martyr* in Greek means "witness." This calling was not merely for those who were killed for their faith but for all believers. Wilken's point is that people normally discover

....
1   Robert Louis Wilken, *The Spirit of Early Christian Thought: Seeking the Face of God* (New Haven: Yale Univ. Press, 2003), 180.

Christ not by listening to dispassionate reports about a past resurrection but by listening to people who experience the risen Lord in his continuing work in their lives. Sometimes these witnesses were called to die for their faith because of persecution, but more often the witnesses were believers who lived in faith amid the usual trials and troubles in a broken, sinful, and hurting world. Being a witness is less often about a romanticized public event and more often about the quiet, ordinary, difficult lives of believers.

As Wilken comments, "Martyrs always speak in the first person."[2] These witnesses spoke about a historical Jesus who walked the roads of Galilee, but even more, they spoke about the risen Lord's present mercies and divine power working in and among them. This power—contrary to expectations—was not so much associated with wealth, political authority, or increased health. Instead, this gospel power was busy with the transforming love of the Father, the life-giving grace of the Son, and the comforting presence of the Spirit.

Given this workaday, anything-but-dramatic picture, how might we serve as faithful witnesses to one another?

One of the things I have learned and valued from the history of the black church in America is the importance they place on the function of witness or "testimony."[3] Whether in response to a preacher or during a small gathering of believers listening to one another, it is not uncommon for saints in the pew to respond to the speaker in the pulpit with phrases like "testify" and "I need a witness." Here the witness normally performs two functions.

First, it affirms the difficulties, trials, or suffering a person is experiencing as real and not imagined. It gives people space to

....
2   Ibid., 181.

3   For helpful background, see Michel Battle, *The Black Church in America: African American Christian Spirituality* (London: Wiley-Blackwell, 2006). For more on the function of witness amid suffering see Kelly M. Kapic, *Embodied Hope: A Theological Meditation on Pain and Suffering* (Downers Grove, IL: IVP Academic, 2017), 152–54.

share what they have experienced and to give voice to their frustrations, fears, and hurts. "This is what is happening and it is so hard."

Second, it affirms God's presence and grace as real and not imagined. It gives those same people courage to speak of the mysterious ways they have seen God show up, bringing comfort, presence, and hope in the hardships. Remarkably, this divine tenderness appears not simply in the absence of the difficulties but even more in their devastating presence. This is the twofold dynamic of serving as a witness.

Whether speaking of a difficult marriage, an unjust landlord, or a debilitating disease, this kind of witness enables listeners to encourage a sister that she is not alone, reassuring her that others see and affirm her difficulties and frustrations. When we are going through tough times like this, we can wonder whether we are crazy, whether we are just imagining that things are so hard. But fellow-pilgrims can help us by listening to our stories and then affirming, "Wow, that is really hard," "I can't believe you are having to face that," or, "You're right, what you are talking about is heartbreaking and I have no solutions."

In this way, without discounting the pain and discouragements, these listeners acknowledge the peculiar ways the believer has experienced God's mercies. Mysterious and sometimes individually personal stories of God's kindness, comfort, and tenderness are welcomed rather than discounted by the faithful. "Yes, that really does sound like God met you in that moment." "Wow, it is amazing how God has provided for you even amid the ongoing challenges."

This tradition that maintains the twofold dynamic of witness has been important throughout the history of the church, from the early Christian martyrs to saints in the black church experience in America.

Such wisdom, however, was not easily gained but usually grew through the fires of pain and suffering. The more affluent side of the American church, not having gone through the same fires, often feels that the unflinching honesty of such witness about the confusion and hurts of life is awkward and alien. We fill our churches with upbeat songs but rarely if ever learn to sing songs of lament. We know how to praise God when things turn out as we wanted, but finding comfort in his presence when our lives turn downward bewilders us, and we often have little guidance or companionship in it. Any view or practice, however, that cannot accept an honest assessment of our pain alongside our hopeful confession of God's goodness and presence goes contrary to the teaching and history of the church. Both can be true. Both are true! But will we listen, or do we sometimes make people choose between them?

Many Christian circles frame the narrative of faith in a way that can lead people to believe that the faithful will escape or overcome every serious difficulty they face. Even if we don't explicitly say such things, our triumphalism becomes obvious in our frustration and impatience, both with ourselves and with others, when life doesn't go as smoothly as we expect. Whether Christians deal with the frustrations of being single despite wanting to be married, or with underemployment in an area that faces chronic job scarcity, when events don't meet our expectations we may start to realize how much we have fused the good news of the gospel with expectations of health, affluence, and consistent success over all difficulties.

But what happens when dire circumstances don't change? What happens when life doesn't turn out as we had hoped? To be honest, what often happens in subtle but almost sinister ways is that we start to blame people. "They are single *because they* . . ." "They face financial difficulties *because they* just don't try hard enough." Yet, such conclusions often come from those who don't know the whole story and have not faced the same situation as the person they are belittling.

Our unexamined assumptions about prosperity and affluence, however, are nowhere more powerfully exposed than when we have to deal with chronic physical pain. We pray for the sick and hurting, asking for God's miraculous healing powers, and it is good and right that we do so. But when the cancer grows rather than disappears, when the soul-crushing pain that we experience doesn't go away after a few days or months even after genuine prayers and belief, when the painful months turn into years and the years turn into decades, we very naturally struggle to know how to respond, how to think about God's goodness in the midst of this unrelenting pain and suffering.

We desperately need these witnesses. We need those who have walked with Jesus not just during the triumphs but during the dark nights of the soul. We need those who have felt like nails were being driven into their skin, day after week after month after year, who even in the ceaseless pain somehow speak of the beauty of Christ, of God's compassion and tender care. Such testimony is what we desperately need, because without it we do not see Jesus clearly, either for ourselves or for others. Hearing that testimony clears our ears to hear the gospel even through the pain and not only apart from it. Hearing it, we gain courage in our faith to face our particular trials and tribulations, our fears and frustrations.

With these comments in mind, I would like to introduce you to a good friend of mine. I remember meeting K.J. as a young college student when she was one of my students. Overflowing with intellectual gifts and physical energy, she was eager and willing to change the world. She worked hard, loved people, and was serious about her faith. It didn't take long to realize she was willing to do hard things for Christ and his kingdom. And then, out of nowhere came pain that was both debilitating and frightening. She didn't know why it was there, where it came from, or whether it would leave. What was she to do? Days turned into months, months turned into years, and now well into her second decade of dealing with chronic pain, I have watched this godly woman testify of God's presence and grace not in any of the ways she hoped or expected, but all the more powerfully, speaking from her weakness rather than strength.

Why should you listen to K.J.? Because she bears witness.

This book is a wonderful example of speaking the truth both about the heartbreaking hardships of life and also about the surprising kindness of our God, who is not distant but personal, present, and active. K.J. does not allow us to pick between being honest about our pain or being attentive to God's goodness. One doesn't choose between these two. One cannot choose between these two. And K.J.'s witness helps us to see that God's compassion, forgiveness, and power are in the midst of our weakness, rather than in its absence.

As she allows us to eavesdrop a bit on her pilgrimage with God, she also provides insights into this God's character. This God is more gracious than you or I tend to imagine. Might it be that this God's vision of the flourishing life differs from ours? Might it be that the good news we speak of is not always accompanied by affluence, health, and power but is genuinely discovered in weakness, need, and dependence?

K.J. is not running from God but has found the wonder of the divine embrace, and she invites us to feel the warmth of our God's presence. As she encourages us to trust this God with our hardships, she also offers us words of courage and kindness. It takes courage to believe God when our lives are filled with hurt. And it takes faith and kindness to derive our true identity and comfort from our connection with him rather than from our ability to produce.

I encourage you to read this book slowly, prayerfully, and with hope. Let her story help you realize you are not alone. And let her testimony of God's kindness in the midst of chronic pain also help you know that the triune God himself is with you and for you. My prayer is that K.J.'s book will help you learn to more confidently rest in the love of the Father, in the grace of the Son, and in the power of the Spirit.

—Dr. Kelly M. Kapic, Professor of Theological Studies, Covenant College

INVITATION

This book is not a before and after story.

I'm writing this introduction as cold immunotherapy drips steadily into my bloodstream to control a disease from which hundreds of people, including myself, have prayed for me to be healed. With an IV in my hand, nausea on my lips, and a roomful of other sick people in my peripheral view, I'm well aware that some diseases aren't healed. Some hard things stay in our lives until Jesus returns, so I'm here to tell a story from the middle, where so many of us live yet so few describe.

⚓

Perhaps like yours, my middle story is messy, and I'm not sure I can bear the mud it has recently smeared over our lives. Today uncertainty and stress are drowning out the sound of the TV while I stare vacantly past my husband's face into our turquoise curtains, the ones I have to pack into a box to put into storage for the second time in a year. We are losing everything, again. Our livelihood, community, and home just evaporated in less than twenty-four hours. I'll leave the explanation of our loss at this: all too often those with the most power have the least awareness of how they wield it, and when this happens in the church, hurt is inevitable. When power blinds people from accounting for their sin, someone else will always foot the bill. In this case, it's my family, and I'm staring absently at the

19

curtains because I'm not sure I can handle the heartbreak of being plundered by the church we've given our entire adult lives to serve.

This is suffering I didn't expect to linger. I set out several months ago to write this book mostly intending to share stories from the past decade of living with an incurable, painful autoimmune disease and the grace that has sustained me along the way. I never imagined that while writing a book about finding grace in suffering, I would feel so bereft of grace because of suffering incurred in the body of Christ herself.

I'm not sure where grace is today, and I snap out of my trance in sudden anger, desperately wanting the thundering pain in my head and heart to be heard. I sling words at the walls and at my husband, Ryan, messy and unapologetically aggressive words, brash strokes telling the darkest story I fear is unfolding. I am honest, and I am hopeless.

Then I'm weeping and empty again, feeling as alone as a leaf floating in the middle of a lake, with no wind to blow me toward shore. I've used all my words, and I know this silence is going to deafen my hope. I'm heading somewhere dark, a mental exile that is hard to return from.

A few hours ago, my husband and I texted an older couple about going over to their house. They are the sole people in our new city, beyond our personal therapists, with whom we have fully shared what is happening.

"They said we can come," Ryan mentions from the other side of the couch.

With the salt of my tears drying and my hopelessness absorbing all the oxygen from our soon-to-be-packed rental house, I feel the smallest swell inside. Ninety-one percent of me doesn't want to go. Ninety-one percent of me doesn't want to recount the rupture of our dreams or let other people hear me hurl my honest faithlessness at the sky. But in ten years of existing with profound pain, I've learned to listen to the 9 percent of me that wants connection as the wisest part of who I am.

So I find myself on a couch facing Tom and Sue with a pile of used tissues accumulating between me and my husband. We're speaking our shock and sharing our tears, perhaps more raw and undignified than you might imagine a pastor and a licensed therapist to be, and they're listening. They're listening long and listening well. Our resounding pain hangs in the sticky silence of the May evening, but rather than dampening hope, this silence amplifies it.

Silence makes space for story.

Tom's face is squirreled in hesitancy. He's telling us about researching his family history and the encouragement he's been finding in the records of his ancestors. He pauses. "I don't want to be trite," he reassures. I can tell he doesn't want to cover our pain with a pretty spiritual bow. Hearing we don't mind, he tells us about his Quaker forebears in colonial Virginia. The British government had passed a law requiring all colonists to have their children baptized in the Church of England, and the punishment for refusal was a fine worth an entire year's wages. Rooted in their convictions, his ancestors paid the fine and absorbed the relational fallout in their community, a great cost that spiraled into years of suffering.

Tom recently procured his ancestors' last will and testament. From the perspective of the end of their lives, they knew that the goodness and grace of God had encompassed their entire lives, including their many years of suffering.

Looking down at my bare feet, I trace the lines of Tom and Sue's Persian rug while listening; its pale blue, rust, and pink are pockets of reprieve for my tear-tired eyes. I look up and nod as Sue says something in reply to Tom. Yes, this is, surprisingly, an encouraging story.

A thought pops into my head: *I'm going to be okay.*

And I know that's why we came, even when I didn't want to,

even though I cursed the body of Christ all the way there, because 9 percent of me knew that it was in her midst that I would find grace. Not grace that fixes our pain. Not grace that rescues. In fact, I still don't know how this new storyline of our lives will work out—how our bills will be paid, how our hearts will mend, or where we'll lay our heads in a month. This is grace for today. Grace that sustains. This is grace that can come only on a couch, through personal presence, with vulnerability on full display.

If my experience of suffering and the stories of the numerous clients I've counseled are any indicator of what your life might include, then you're likely also midstory in circumstances you did not choose, wondering when and how your suffering will end and where grace will come if it doesn't.

Our society loves tales of rising heroes. We've so fused our American Dream with the risen Christ that when suffering enters our lives and does not leave quickly, all we know how to do is hide, judge, or despair. We've reduced the gospel to rescue, power to privilege, and hope to swift healing, reducing ourselves in the process. Western Christendom has long treated suffering like a problem to fix and a blight to hide. Eugene Peterson was right: "It is difficult to find anyone in our culture who will respect us when we suffer."[1] When our storylines do not match the arc of triumph we've come to expect and revere, we can feel stuck on the outside of both our communities and God's grace.

You don't need another before and after story; you need grace for the middle of your story.

If you are hoping to learn how to save yourself from your

....
1   Eugene H. Peterson, *A Long Obedience in the Same Direction: Discipleship in an Instant Society* (Downers Grove, IL: InterVarsity Press, 2000), 138.

suffering, this book is going to disappoint you. If you want to be impermeable to pain, this book will probably make you mad. If you are looking for easy tips to move from groaning to glory, you might just want to give your copy away right now. But if you, like me, keep finding that all the faith you can muster won't push your suffering over the edge of the cliff into your past, then I'd like to invite you to sit down at that fearsome ledge instead.

All I have to offer you is an invitation.

In these pages is my outstretched hand. Instead of claiming to have solutions, I'm inviting you to sit in the places where I've found sustaining grace, grace that is upholding me even now while my world seems to fall apart yet again. I'm no rising hero; I'm a chronically ill thirty-one-year-old who in the last decade has spent more hours sick on a couch than standing in the workforce. But it's on couches, through tears, that I've come to see that living with suffering that lingers can mean more fully receiving God's presence that lasts.

Come sit on my couch at the ledge, just like I've sat on countless couches across from my spouse, friends, therapists, pastors, and clients. You're not on the outside here. Settle in. Push up the pillows just how you like them. Wrap that blanket over your legs. You might not feel comfortable yet, but I know there's grace for you here.

I can't offer a way to make your pain past-tense, but I can offer my presence. I won't make you hide your hard things. Tears and expletives are welcome here. It's difficult to look suffering in the face, and throughout this book we will name our hard things with courage, and sometimes it might make you squirm. But with my words of all the ways I've been sustained in a story I never would have chosen, I hope you'll feel a greater Presence sustaining you.

Maybe you don't know if this couch is for you. Maybe you don't think your hard things are hard enough to matter, or perhaps you picked up this book to help someone else. This couch is for you too. You are more than welcome here. As you thumb through these pages, you'll encounter something you may not like but do need: the truth that the weakness hidden in the hollows of your soul is the place where God wants to show his strength. To be human is to be vulnerable, and I think you'll find your story in these pages as well.

Together, seated on what some might call a sideline, we'll witness a mystery illuminated.

We'll find that the pain we wish we could end, the pain most books on suffering promise to turn into a shiny transformation story, is actually the place we can encounter the most grace. Seated by the ledge where we've exhausted ourselves trying to push away suffering, we'll see that pain embraced and accepted provides a panoramic perspective of the dawning of God's new world.

We'll watch for the dawn while acknowledging the dark. And as the black and blue of night recede with the radiance of the rising sun, we'll realize we're in the company of Jesus.

On the couch by the ledge, in a place most Christians want to rush right past on their way to glory, we'll see glimpses of a glory already with us. We'll encounter a truth best seen seated: that the greatest story ever told is of a God who so loved the world that he chose to suffer for it. We'll see what we can't see when we're busy searching for the purpose in our pain or hustling hard to prove how valuable we are for God's kingdom. Suffering has always been God's means of rousing a sleeping world with his love.[2]

The world will keep shouting at us to stand, jeering and leering that weakness is shame, but Love already came to the couch to sit in the place of our pain. While the world has always worshiped strength, God chose weakness to display his love. The spectacle of God's love was never power or prestige but descent. And it's those who wear the spectacles of tears who best glimpse this beautiful

----

2   C. S. Lewis writes, "Pain insists upon being attended to. God whispers to us in our pleasures, speaks in our conscience, but shouts in our pain: it is His megaphone to rouse a deaf world." C. S. Lewis, *The Problem of Pain* (New York: HarperOne, 1996), 92.

descent. God became human, with blood that would spill and a heart that would break, to unite us to love that lasts. The One with power gave it up so that in our powerlessness we could know his presence.

Somehow it's when we're seated instead of standing, well aware of our lack of strength, that we can most clearly see his. Because Jesus chose weakness, it's where we can receive strength. Suffering can be the place we wake up to the power and presence of Christ.

So listen to this more closely than to those who taunt or judge, including yourself: "God has chosen what is foolish in the world to shame the wise, and God has chosen what is weak in the world to shame the strong. God has chosen what is insignificant and despised in the world."[3] The parts of your story that seem to be keeping you from strength and significance are what God calls chosen and valuable. If you keep turning the pages of this book, maybe by the end you will too.

Here on the couch, I'll tell you a story truer than my pain, greater than my woes, and more lasting than all that is disappointing you. You'll see the surprising truth that the parts of our stories we most fear—and even most hate—are the places we can most be enfolded into God's lasting story of love. We'll find that the body of Christ holds the grace we need when suffering lingers—grace embodied in the life of Jesus, who chose to absorb all the pain we cannot handle, and his abiding presence in us by his Spirit and with us through his people, imperfect though they may be. We'll learn that our brains and bodies were always meant to flourish in relationships, and that suffering invites us to sit in the space where we can be made whole. Grace exists in the space between us.

I pray that the space between us in these pages makes grace as tangible as the paper on which these words are printed. I pray that the small space we share through these chapters reveals the

....
3   1 Cor. 1:27-28.

larger space within you, around you, and underneath you where God's grace is more present than we can imagine. And I pray that seated together on the couch of this shared story, we both behold the sacred mystery of Christ in us, the hope of glory. The beauty of the dawn will overcome this night.

And one day soon, we will rise. We'll trade our places on this couch for honored seats around a table. We'll sit, with bodies that no longer ache and minds that no longer fear, and instead of pain, we'll share laughter. The tears we needed to glimpse grace will be wiped away by Christ's tender, scarred hands. And we'll watch with wonder as God hurls death like a fireball into a fathomless sea, never again to be seen. Wrapped in the bright linen of our perseverance, we'll see earth and heaven newborn. And from the silent spaces of sorrow within and between us will rise the most stunning song.

Glory will be our sun. Joy will be our inheritance. God will be our king.

With his words of "well done" still ringing in our ears, we'll look at each other with smiles and see. This couch was a throne all along.

CHAPTER 1

DISSONANCE

The Clash of Suffering in a Crescendo Culture

> For grace to be grace, it must give us things we didn't
> know we needed and take us to places where we
> didn't want to go. As we stumble through the crazily
> altered landscape of our lives, we find that God is
> enjoying our attention as never before.
>
> —KATHLEEN NORRIS, *ACEDIA AND ME*

I was wearing red pajamas with printed Valentine candy hearts the day I learned pain does not always elicit help. I don't particularly like candy hearts, but that day I was too tired to dress myself. So I arrived at the University of Michigan rheumatology office with an unkempt combination of unbrushed hair, my favorite college sweatshirt, and pajamas from the restless night before. Not even two weeks earlier, my body had effortlessly climbed tree-lined trails, exhaustion a pleasant reward on the way to more adventures. Now I could barely hold myself up, fatigue crumpling my body into a curled lump on the crinkly-papered exam table.

This body was unfamiliar. I only knew myself as fierce, capable, and strong, not the weakened ball lying in the fetal position in a specialist's office 615 miles from the college where I was living my dreams. I lay there in pain, in a body that had been sick only about six times in its twenty rotations around the sun, at once hopeful about the help I would receive and fearful about the way I sensed my life might be changing forever.

I did not know then that pain cannot always be treated effectively. I did not know that women in pain are often regarded with suspicion by doctors.[1] I still occupied a reality where the proper response to suffering was empathy, not the cold, sterile world of ugly chairs in poorly decorated waiting rooms leading to smaller rooms of prodding, pushing, and questioning, followed by pricks of pain to fill vials with blood, carried away by people who wanted to know my name only to check against the charts that would become thick as encyclopedias in the years to come.

There was so much I didn't know.

I was sick enough that the rheumatologist promptly ordered enough bloodwork to fill fourteen vials. I was sick enough to be ushered down the hallway to other specialists of things I did not know existed, to rule out diseases I had never heard of. But this would not be enough. My parents, who had rescued me from college a week before, now helped me walk down the fluorescent-lit hallways, hobbling past the jarring sight of wheelchairs I hoped I wouldn't need. There was an odd, pungent smell of synthetic citrus soap mixed with a faint hint of decay. Dizzy from the blood draw, I made it back to the rheumatology office. But this time the doctor came with another, whom she introduced as a first-year resident. Then she turned around and left the room, allowing the resident to proceed with the appointment on his own.

....

1   See Ashley Fetters, "The Doctor Doesn't Listen to Her. But the Media Is Starting To," *The Atlantic* (August 10, 2018), *www.theatlantic.com/family/archive/2018/08/womens-health-care-gaslighting/567149/*; Joe Fassler, "How Doctors Take Women's Pain Less Seriously," *The Atlantic* (October 15, 2015), *www.theatlantic.com/health/archive/2015/10/emergency-room-wait-times-sexism/410515/*.

In a world where most people are relieved to not get bad news, I quickly learned the devastation of no news. I was told my blood-work had come back negative, a word I found more disappointing than comforting. The resident, who was barely older than me but clothed with the power of the white coat, began pressing my body for trigger points. From my quick online research, I had learned this was the definitive test for fibromyalgia, a disorder characterized by symptoms different from mine, a disorder that is sometimes thought to be psychosomatic.[2] After the exam I sat down with my arms folded tight, safe in the cocoon of my college sweatshirt, and realized for the first time that young women in unexplainable pain are often considered mentally unstable. I recoiled in defense, instantly aware my pain and body had been misjudged.

Finding no proof of the pain drawing my hands into fists and my back into an unpleasant stoop, the resident had stopped listening to my pleas for help. That day, I started carrying the grief of my inconvenient body, sick but not sick enough to be easily diagnosed, desperate but not dying, suffering but unseen.

Finally, the rheumatologist returned, and only after hearing the insistent desperation of my parents, she prescribed the first of what would become more than fifty medications I would try in the coming decade to treat the pain one doctor thought was all in my head.

At twenty years old, with pain that could not be validated by a blood test or an X-ray, I began to feel less like a person full of

2   At the time of this appointment in 2009, fibromyalgia was, even more than today, experienced by many female patients as a catch-all diagnosis when a doctor was suspicious of one's pain having a physical origin. I am in no way calling fibromyalgia a primarily psychosomatic disorder. Rather, it is a complex disorder in which one's central nervous system causes widespread pain. As you will learn throughout this book, I believe *all* pain is embodied and real, a conclusion I have found through both science and the crucible of my own pain being disbelieved and minimized by medical professionals.

potential and more like a number and a burden. This is primarily why suffering scares us, because it makes us feel like we are becoming less than human.[3] If suffering lingers, when pain and disorders and grief stretch into years instead of lasting for days or months, we fear we will lose our very selves.

Pain threatens personhood.

Whether the pain that prompted you to pick up this book is physical, emotional, spiritual, relational, or psychological, it triggers the same neurobiological process.[4] Pain—of all origins—is almost instantly processed in our brains and bodies as a threat to our existence. Because of this, when I use the word pain throughout this book, I want it to prompt you to reflect on the hard things in *your* life. When I refer to pain, I am speaking inclusively of all the stinging losses and sharp edges in our lives. From disease to depression, from grief to spiritual longing, from anxiety to trauma, all our weaknesses and struggles involve real pain carried and expressed in our real bodies. Remembering that your pain matters and is embodied will be like a compass, guiding you home to your body in your story as you journey through this book.

The moment we feel pain, our bodies instinctively pulse to protect themselves, and they struggle to do much else as our brains focus their energy and attention on survival. We feel less like ourselves and less connected to others when in pain, because pain itself prompts a "sensation of internal disintegration."[5] Our bodies intuitively shut down and shut others out to survive, making it incredibly difficult to access the parts of our brains that help us

....

3   Anatole Broyard writes, "It may not be dying we fear so much, but the diminished self." Quoted in Arthur W. Frank, *The Wounded Storyteller: Body, Illness, and Ethics* (Chicago: Univ. of Chicago Press, 2013), 39.

4   Peter A. Moskovitz, "Understanding Suffering: The Phenomenology and Neurobiology of the Experience of Illness and Pain," in *Maldynia: Multidisciplinary Perspectives on the Illness of Chronic Pain,* ed. James Giordano (Boca Raton, FL: CRC, 2016), 34.

5   Clara Costa Oliveira, "Understanding Pain and Human Suffering," *Revista Bioética* 24, no. 2 (2016): 225–34.

think rationally, keep perspective, and feel secure in our relationships. Social connectedness and pain are so intertwined, they share the same neurobiological pathway.[6] When pain of any kind makes us feel less ourselves and less capable of engaging in relationships, we experience it as suffering.[7] Feeling out of sorts and unlike yourself when in pain isn't your fault. It's an automatic, natural consequence of living in a body.

Suffering is coming to the edge of ourselves, to the place where we viscerally feel the truth that being human is being limited. All pain triggers a reminder, deeper than thought, buzzing through blood and bone, that we are fragile and finite. Suffering whispers, shouts, and screams the story no one wants to remember: we are not in control, and we are all going to die.

Suffering places our bodies and stories in tension with the story we've been soaking up our entire lives. The drumbeat of Western culture is that effort produces success. With enough foresight and determination, we each can create a life with minimal pain and maximum pleasure. We are proprietors of possibility, the doorkeepers of our own bright futures. Our bodies are vehicles of productivity, a currency that purchases success or an inconvenience that impedes it. With hands over our hearts, we pledge allegiance to the red, white, and blue ideal of an autonomous, uninhibited life of safety and ease. If we try hard enough, we will triumph.

The unspoken story of Western culture is that suffering is a problem we can avoid or annihilate if we work hard enough. When suffering lingers, we feel we have failed to reach the allegedly reachable American Dream. Held in the invisible grip of this story, lives including pain are problems to fix. So we march our bodies to the beat of progress, resolved to fight back the darkness that's keeping us from the achievement and enjoyment we feel is rightfully

....
6   Kirsten Weir, "The Pain of Social Rejection," *American Psychological Association* 43, no. 4 (2012): 50.
7   Moskovitz, "Understanding Suffering," 34–61.

ours. We're God's children, after all. Doesn't he want us to be well? Doesn't he want us to show the world the resurrection is real?

Living in a story where suffering lingers makes us aware of the clash between the false music filling and forming our lives and the tune of the God who says he is good. The slowing of our bodies, the breaking of our marriages, and the shattering of our lives through abuse change the way we hear the background music that has been permeating our existence. All our lives, we have marched to the cadence of a culture that tells us we can avoid suffering through hard work. With a body that cannot work or a spirit crushed by loss, we feel like flat notes played a beat behind in a song whose tempo no longer feels achievable. Living with long-term suffering in American culture feels like being off-key. Suffering quiets and slows, but our culture prefers a crescendo.

When the notes of your life are in a minor key of somber limitation, you come to hear the sounds of shame screeching and scraping in all our lives under the pulsing beat of progress. Most people silence shame reflexively with busyness. If every moment of the day is full of the sounds of cars, drive-through lines, and paper pushing, we won't have to hear the echo chamber of our worst fears. We hide in hurry, working hard to align our lives with the pulsating pace we sense everyone else is living at. The music blasting in our ears is energetic and bright, and without thinking, we ignore or shove away anything that doesn't match the sounds of success. When suffering becomes chronic, no matter how good we are at numbing, we will hear the sounds of shame turning us into less than ourselves. As Kathleen Norris has expressed, "Our busyness can't disguise the suspicion that we are being steadily diminished, not so much living as passing time in a desert of our own devising."[8]

We live in a conqueror culture, vultures preying on weakness,

....
8   Kathleen Norris, *Acedia and Me: A Marriage, Monks, and a Writer's Life* (New York: Penguin, 2008), 132.

fixed on gnawing our sorrows into stories of success. If we can't protect ourselves from pain, we'll overcome it. We'll search high and low for its purpose, and having found it, we'll show the world God's strength.

Even this effort exhausts us, bringing us back to the barren ground of being in bodies that won't do what we wish they would in lives that don't look like we wish they would look. And if what we hear from God's people is largely the language of try hard and triumph, the sugar-lipped expectation that we'll get better and move on, when our efforts are futile and triumph seems distant, we might just believe that the story of Jesus isn't for us or isn't even true. Prolonged pain becomes shame, a hidden hurt that we might not be loved by God after all.

As we seek to make pain and weakness past-tense, the sweat of our effort blurs our vision of the goodness and grace that might already be here. With our attention aimed at finding a silver lining, our minds simply don't have room to experience our actual lives in our actual bodies as valuable and worthwhile. We remain allergic to our actual lives, addicted to maintaining an illusion of control, desperate to whip our bodies and stories into submission to the story of self-sufficiency and the glory we think it affords.

Of course, none of us want to admit this.

None of us want to acknowledge the silent sin lacing the water we drink and offer each other. No one wants to face the fact that we live like self-appointed dictators over disembodied kingdoms, demanding happiness, safety, and security. When we don't get the pain-free, protected lives we want, it hurts. It haunts. It opens our eyes and hearts to the truth: we aren't God, and trying to be won't give us what we thought we wanted.

The pain of no longer fitting into our culture's story of success is immense. The sorrow of feeling betrayed by the bodies we thought would work better and work longer is serious. The loneliness of realizing there's a weakness inside us that no amount of effort or faith can eradicate makes us feel like exiles. Living with suffering that lingers can feel like being an unwanted refugee in a country blind to pain. You feel outside grace, outside light, out of reach of what you think makes life good. Your body holds a story quite different than the story your culture says is worth living. And you're not sure you want to, or even can, move forward with this body in this story.

In the story of our culture, the story driven by shame, suffering does not make sense beyond the scope of individual failure. But the losses that compelled you to pick up this book were likely not the consequence of dismal choices. This is why you are angry. This is why you shudder and spiral, even if you mostly do so within the privacy of your own home, where no one can see or judge. Where do you hang the weight of what ails you? Without remembering a bigger story, we hang the shame of suffering on ourselves and on God, rejecting our bodies, our current lives, and sometimes our faith as sources of disappointment.

The story of Scripture shows where our self-rejection, striving, and turning away from God originate. Further, within the story of God and his good, loved creation, we find our pain has a place in the plot that is neither final nor entirely our fault. Only within this bigger story can we face our real sin and shame and find the burden of brokenness lifted and shaped into something beautiful.

God spoke the world into being, from the molecules forming water to the pine tree that sways in the wind outside my window. He called it good. But when God made humans, he breathed us into being. From the dirt of the ground, he formed a reflection of himself. Humanity—the reflection of God formed from dirt. He called us good, very good indeed.

Our story begins as dust made matter, breathed out of the

overflow of love between the Father, Son, and Holy Spirit, and named very good. Our story begins in joyful communion with God and dominion over his world. We were naked and felt no shame.[9]

God gave Adam and Eve purpose, provision, and relationship to fill the earth with the abundance of his blessing. "Look at what I have given you," he said, pointing out the plants he formed from nothing and dreamed up with care to innately replicate and reproduce as plentiful food.[10] God made food and fruit for feasting and filling. But one tree was off-limits. In Fatherly care, God instructed Adam that he must not eat from the tree of the knowledge of good and evil, telling him that if he did, he would die.[11] God gave boundaries to Adam and Eve out of love, creating a well-defined place to flourish.

In the lush garden, while goodness lingered and flowed from every living thing, a serpent slithered onto the scene, tricking the first couple into questioning God's trustworthiness and kindness. The serpent aroused fear in Eve, leveraging her left brain's capacity to analyze by considering right from wrong, evoking the emotional experience of distress.[12] The tide of all history turned in the conversation between the serpent and Eve, as the serpent twisted God's words of provision and protection into words of malicious intent to withhold good from the children he supposedly loved.

Eve wanted what wasn't given. She wanted the wisdom hidden in the tree, the knowledge of good and evil, an awareness that was bigger than her body could hold. By the end of the serpent's exchange with Eve, she took the only fruit God had instructed them to not eat, and both she and Adam were left naked and ashamed.

Sin and shame disrupt the human story, diminishing the spaces

....

9 Gen. 2:25.
10 Gen. 1:29-30, my paraphrase.
11 Gen. 2:17.
12 Curt Thompson, *Anatomy of the Soul: Surprising Connections between Neuroscience and Spiritual Practices That Can Transform Your Life and Relationships* (Carol Stream, IL: Tyndale, 2010), 207-8.

between us, reducing them from communion to separation. Shame defeats the human story, igniting doubt about how loved we are by God and turning us away from the One who provides to attempt to provide for ourselves. Self-sufficiency is our first response to shame and suffering. Realizing their nakedness, Adam and Eve tried to cover their exposure, sewing together fig leaves for themselves and hiding from God when they realized he was near.[13] God doesn't turn from those he loves, and he came to find Adam and Eve. He pursued them, even after they disobeyed. He did not turn away from their shame.

"Who told you that you were naked?" he asked,[14] offering an opportunity to acknowledge how the conversation between the serpent and Eve provoked their terrible exposure. God's questions invited the possibility of repair, of connection.[15] But Adam responded to God by doing what shame often stirs us to do— blaming someone else. Blamed before her Maker, Eve continued the cycle of shame by pointing her finger at the serpent. Instead of responding to God's invitation to be known in what they did, the first humans put up a relational barrier between themselves and God by blaming, deflecting, and disowning.

Our human stories of striving, self-rejection, and hiding from ourselves, others, and God all originate in the garden. So does our suffering. God keeps his promises, and his promise of the consequences of eating the fruit has stood.[16] Death now lines every strand of our DNA. Decay is in every body, every story. Every relationship

---

13 Gen. 3:7–8.
14 Gen. 3:11.
15 Thompson, *Anatomy of the Soul*, 218.
16 Gen. 2:17. The curse of the fall touches everything. Theologian Michael Williams writes, "God imposes a series of curses on the participants of the first sin: the serpent whose temptation occasioned the sin, Eve, and then Adam. He expels the man and woman from the Garden. Henceforth they and their posterity will experience the world as an inhospitable place, a place of toilsome labor and great danger." Michael D. Williams, *Far as the Curse Is Found: The Covenant Story of Redemption* (Phillipsburg, NJ: Presbyterian and Reformed, 2005), 67.

is cracked and crumbling from holding more than it was made to hold. Our relationships with God, ourselves, the created world, and one another are fractured by sin.[17]

Like Adam and Eve, we continue to reach for a life beyond our bounds. The desire to be limitless is our original sin.

Just like the first humans, we want what we do not have and reject what we've been given. We don't want the bodies we have. We don't want the history that's shaped us. We don't want the stories we are living. We don't want our shame to be seen.

So we reach. Like Eve, we want a wisdom too big for our bodies to hold. We desperately desire the knowledge of good and evil, the secret sagacity that would make our hurt make sense. Since God isn't giving us what we want, we try to get it on our own. We try to be self-sufficient, to find the purpose in our pain, to create the relief we long for, and to get back to enjoying what seems delightful. Except we don't call it sin. We call it "redeeming what is broken" and "creating beauty from ashes." Instead of living fully within the borders of the lives we've been given, we plot an escape and call it faith.

Sin is the echo of Eve, inclining us to name our bodies and their limitations as bad. Sin is the shadow of the serpent, tempting us to believe God is less than he says he is and will provide far less than he has promised.

Oddly enough, many of us learn the sin of disembodied self-sufficiency in church. We're a people formed around worshiping the God who so loved us embodied people that he became one of us, but we treat our bodies with suspicion and contempt instead of sacred awe. Our bodies are temples of the Holy Spirit, but we often

....
17 Bryant L. Myers, *Walking with the Poor: Principles and Practices of Transformational Development* (Maryknoll, NY: Orbis, 2009), 27.

see them more like burning receptacles of Satan's power. We learn from childhood to mistrust our bodies, minimize our emotions, and elevate the mind as the seat of all that is sacred. As Christian philosopher James K. A. Smith has noted, Christian worship, education, and worldview formation have long treated humans as primarily thinking beings.[18] We are so much more than walking heads.[19]

We live with the inheritance of thousands of years of handling our bodies like past, present, and future crime sites, misinterpreting Scripture's understanding of the flesh to be all that is physical. Without realizing it, we approach ourselves and others with a religious sword, splitting ourselves in two, the physical and the spiritual, demeaning the physical as a separate part opposed to worship, faith, and joy. We look at our whole bodies, whole stories, and whole selves that God made and called very good, and we unwittingly call part of them very bad.

While sin has tainted every atom of creation and every plot line of our stories, God's original declaration of us as good remains. Further, Goodness himself took on flesh to dwell among us, forever affirming human bodies in human stories as the place where God reveals his love. But we approach our bodies and physical experiences like prisons trapping our souls, denying them their higher, spiritual destinies. It turns out it's not just our culture that treats bodies like commodities or inconveniences in service of success. Christians do too. We just call it holiness. We treat our physical experiences like the snare keeping us from joy, separating us from God. When so much around us has taught us to regard our bodies with either doubt and scorn or perfectionistic preoccupation, how can we look at suffering as anything other than a short-term problem to solve as quickly as possible?

....

18 James K. A. Smith, *Desiring the Kingdom (Cultural Liturgies): Worship, World-view, and Cultural Formation* (Grand Rapids: Baker Academic, 2009).
19 Brad D. Strawn and Warren S. Brown, "Liturgical Animals: What Psychology and Neuroscience Tell Us about Formation and Worship," *Liturgy* 28, no. 4 (2013): 3.

Similarly, when bodies are prisons and the physical is suspect, how can we ever encounter pain as a meaningful experience or, shockingly, the place where God comes to find us, a physical experience he chose to go through himself to bind us to his life?

◆

When I first got sick, I was asked about unrepentant sin. Surely, some secret attitude, behavior, or pattern was causing my suffering. I racked my brain for answers. If I could find the hidden sin and repent, then maybe the suffering would cease. What lesson was God trying to teach me? If I could learn it, maybe I would stop hurting.

Contrary to how many Christians approach hard things, suffering is often not an indication of hidden sin or evidence of a lack of faith. What if the real sin is to witness suffering and immediately judge the sufferer as bad? Sin is letting our pernicious anxiety make us blame someone for the suffering we see. Sin is seeing weakness and assuming its bearer lacks faith. Sin is expecting ourselves and others to be miniature self-saviors who can rise above our broken bodies and broken stories and eliminate suffering by the power of our own determined truth-telling.

Sin is calling a failure what is actually the fall. It's forgetting our origin story, the sin of self-sufficiency, and the outcome of living beyond the boundaries of what God has given. It's forgetting that every part of creation cries out because of the curse. It's forgetting that broken bodies, broken stories, and broken relationships are the result of ancient sin. It's personalizing what are often bigger consequences of a massive story. Disease, disorders, weakness, poverty, and grief are the losing legacy of humanity, the shards of sin shattering us, from the smallest cell to the largest cultural system. The Savior came and is coming again, but our healing is in *his* hands, not our own. If our Savior chose to enter the human story in a human body, then we should enter one another's places of suffering remembering we carry and extend the presence of Christ. Sin is any Christian's response to pain, poverty, and weakness that assumes they are individual problems to solve rather than places to patiently embody the solidarity of Jesus.

When we reduce pain to an individual problem, we don't know what to do with ourselves and our stories. In an increasingly individualistic society, where the space between self, tradition, and our embodied connection to each other feels wide, suffering can be a massive assault to our sense of self and our ability to hope. We become lost in a chasm of overspiritualized pain and undervalued physicality, not knowing where our lives fit alongside a Christianity glittering with the veneer of abundance. Already exhausted, we sink under the weight of existing as an aberration of the abundant life our Christian friends and families want us to project. Defeated and lonely, many of us subconsciously attempt to detach from the grief in our bodies, excising it from our minds to feel accepted in the community of the able and successful. We push pain away with effort, pretending to be okay among the shiny, smiling faces at church or work. For if we were honest about how sad or sick or hopeless we really feel, would we be accepted at all?

There is a widening gap between expressing our faith individually and rooting that faith in community, a gap that leaves us with inadequate shared language to draw from to describe the turmoil of prolonged suffering.[20] A poverty of shared language leads to poverty of hope. We don't have language for lament because we don't view weakness as an expected reality. We don't have space to grieve, because we're too busy judging grief or seeking

....

20 As *New York Times* columnist David Brooks writes, "The grand narrative of individual emancipation left us with what some have called 'the great disembedding.'" Individualism has steadily severed us from the committed fabric of relationship and institutional rhythms and norms that could tether us to meaning and hope when life is shifting and scary. David Brooks, *The Second Mountain: The Quest for a Moral Life* (New York: Random House, 2019), 31.

its relief to speak its truth aloud. As a therapist, I've known many Christian clients whose faith buckles under the weight of displacement from a story, language, and community large enough to hold suffering's tension. With less and less biblical literacy and connection to church, sufferers are untethered from the language, narrative, and practices that could anchor us in understanding, encouragement, and hope.

We feel ashamed of our suffering and confused about its role in our lives because the story we've been handed disowns grief and minimizes weakness. We struggle to accept and cope with suffering because our culture tells us to deny or hide it. Our silence and pretending is the inheritance of Christians who have so swallowed the American Dream we have lost sight of our suffering Lord.

Growing up in an evangelical church and attending a small Christian school, I digested a steady diet of disembodied hope. Though I suspected and secretly hoped the object of Christian faith was not floating on a cloud, singing terrible worship music for the remainder of my existence, no one offered me a more sensible alternative. The language of sin and heaven seemed inadequate, even before physical suffering entered my life, especially because many of the Christians I knew seemed at best sad and at worst hypocritical. I didn't realize it, but I was longing for joy in a subculture striving for perfection. Joy's absence had subconsciously fueled my search for meaning, but striving had carved well-worn routes into the pathways of my brain.

My first years at Covenant College anchored my faith in the more compelling and whole story of the God who came in the flesh to redeem and restore instead of burn and judge. When I first visited the church that would become my home during my college years, I felt something in the sea of swaying, clapping bodies I had only sampled in other Christian communities.[21] In movement, song, and diversity, I encountered enthralling, refreshing joy. Pieces of my faith that had been disembodied and fragmented began to fit within the arc of a bigger story and an incarnate body, Jesus Christ and his church.

But learning a story and believing that story when everything in us quakes and hurts are two different things. So when sickness invaded my strong body as a college junior and then didn't leave, I had to believe something. And I found my way to belief, and even joy, but only through the pain of shedding dense layers of individualistic striving.

The church where I had tasted joy became difficult to get to with my new, weaker body. My hands couldn't quite grasp the steering wheel of my beloved green truck, so I had to find rides down the ambling roads of Lookout Mountain to make it to church in the city below. The chemotherapy pills I had started soon after that initial doctor's appointment made me nauseated, so the winding road was difficult to tolerate. Once at church, I was embarrassed by the trail of hair I left behind in every seat, my body struggling to receive the poison sold to it as medicine. I was confused by the way tears would unexpectedly come when we'd sing, the lyrics touching a wound deep inside that needed healing and a hope that needed air.

When we sang of lifting our hands, hearts, and eyes to the hills, where our help comes from, my tears were prayer and praise. Lifting hands that couldn't work well enough to get me to church without help, a heart trembling in uncertainty and weighed down by dismissal, and eyes unaccustomed to seeing the weak body staring back in the mirror, I began to sense the mixture of longing and nearness that would mark the next decade of my life. Even now I struggle to name it, an odd amalgam of pain and yearning touched by a sense of love.

....
21 During college I attended New City Fellowship in Chattanooga, Tennessee, a multicultural church focused on "producing discipled believers who become God's instruments of grace, justice, and mercy." *www.newcityfellowship.com.*

Weeks after my trip to the University of Michigan rheumatology office, I sat in the dark on top of my dorm bed on a floral quilt of yellow, green, and blue, alone with a body too sick to leave bed. Leaning against the cold cinderblock wall to hold myself up, I tried and failed to open my Bible. The hands that had, with my mom's, pieced together the tiny triangles of the quilt I sat on couldn't handle the basic pinch and lift of turning a single page of Scripture. I couldn't even open the books that held the currency of my connection to God and others. I couldn't care for anyone else, write a paper, or study for a test. All the ways we learn to show we are worthwhile can evaporate.

All my life, I'd subconsciously believed a story of strength—that independent striving was the narrator of success. Sickness killed the narrator, or at least left him fatally wounded. My whole life had been an unfurling series of achievements shielding me from hurt, trauma, and loneliness. Suffering cut through my exterior of exceptionalism, exposing the self beneath my striving.

I had nothing to offer God but my broken heart and broken body.

We wonder who we will encounter when our armor falls off. Will we even recognize ourselves? We fear the silent alone, where no work, capability, or activity can define our value. Many of us live with eyes closed tight against our suffering and the suffering of others because we're terrified of our sin and selves being dissolved. We fear looking long at our pain, because we think if we start looking, we may never see anything else. A reluctance to see only adds the burden of daily pretending to already-present daily pain. An unwillingness to see our real, broken bodies and strained stories keeps us from becoming the people we truly are—people more loved by God than we can realize or feel when we're busy protecting ourselves from pain.

All pain matters. All pain impacts our whole selves. All pain needs a story and response greater than the dualistic sludge covering our eyes, preventing us from seeing our true suffering and true Lord.

What if we've been desperately, unconsciously seeking a story that isn't even good?

What if self-sufficiency was always a bankrupt lie, and suffering simply demonstrates its poverty?

What if suffering isn't ruining our selves but re-creating them?

Suffering is an invitation to live and tell the story truer and more satisfying than pain-free ease. It is an invitation to know and be known by the God who entered the human story intent on transforming death into life. The presence of prolonged suffering begs us to remember our true story and its suffering Lord.

We whose suffering is inconvenient, mysterious, and threatening to both ourselves and those around us are held and loved by a God who not only sees our inadequacy but injected himself into it by taking on human flesh.

Pain and suffering disrupt our relationships and disintegrate our bodies, down to the very functioning of our neurons, but God calls us good and loved. When we choose to live open-eyed, when we allow our suffering, weakness, and unarmored selves to be seen by God, ourselves, and others, we may find there was goodness in these stories of suffering all along.

We need a story bigger than success. We need incarnation. We need embodiment. We need exposure and sight and light that touches darkness in actual bodies, with real histories, in the places where we most want rescue, relief, and retribution.

This is a story where pain propels communion. It's the most surprising, curious, and true story of all, where the Author—God himself—not only tells the story but enters it and changes everything, not by winning but by suffering.

In Jesus, this is what we have. Not the stories we thought we wanted but the one we most need.

This story is mine, and it is yours. Come, let us find the grace that is here.

CHAPTER 2

WARRING STORYLINES

Hijacked by Shame, Healed by Solidarity

*Realize who God is, what he has done, who you are
in Christ, where history is going. Put your troubles
in perspective by remembering Christ's troubles on
your behalf, and all his promises to you, and what he
is accomplishing.*

—TIM KELLER, *WALKING WITH GOD
THROUGH PAIN AND SUFFERING*

The roaring rainstorm sweeping northern Wyoming seized my attention as we drove to our temporary landing place of Bozeman, Montana. Gripping the wheel and staring hard through the curtain of rain coming across the windshield, I slowly adjusted to the storm we were in. By the time I saw an incoming call from a dear friend, I was calm enough to answer. Lore had faced sorrows like our own, sorrows like the one that had us jobless, homeless, and driving up I-25 with all our earthly possessions in a five-by-eight U-Haul trailer in search of solace and a future. As the torrent receded into a drizzle, I trickled out the story of our most recent suffering, primly summarizing in the plainest terms how more hard things had happened.

"You need to let your pain matter," she responded. "Don't rush to make everything sound more okay than it is."

I'd spoken these same words to dozens of my therapy clients, but hearing them was like rain in a drought. Hydration hurts a little when you're cracked and trying to keep yourself from crumbling. Her voice and presence were a tender dressing on a wound that had just started healing, the kind of dressing you can't change on your own.

My mouth had said there were blessings in disguise, but my body was tense with the truth of its discouragement. I was tired of sharing stories of suffering. I was ashamed of having one more hard thing happen, afraid my friends would eventually blame me for all the suffering in my life. So I simplified, minimizing our present pain into a pittance of what it actually was. Lore heard past my words, reminding me that patient honesty is better than shamed silence or withheld woes.

I want to live in the equidistant place between truth and sorrow, the place where pain dwells companionably with mystery. And sometimes that means refusing to plaster an overlay of tidy goodness on my experiences. It means letting someone hear I'm crumbling, weak, and weary. Sometimes hope comes through sight, in showing the truth our bodies are telling about our stories instead of placing pretty words of purpose over our pain. Sometimes the most faithful response to suffering is letting ourselves show our honest sadness.

After I hung up the phone, I wondered if this is the surprising way of Jesus, the man who so fully honored our pain that he took it into his very body and carried it to the cross. I wondered if his is a story we can't fully remember on our own, if it takes phone calls and gentle prodding to be honest and be seen to spot through the rushing storms of today that our stories are *still* part of his.

I wondered if finding grace when suffering lingers requires moving from hiding to honest, from naked to clothed, from withholding and ashamed in our singular stories of suffering to being held in a shared story of God's solidarity with our pain.

Deep down, our greatest fear is that if we express how broken and scared we really feel, we will sink into complete darkness. We fear that expressing the depth of our discouragement will separate us from God. This is the knife edge of shame in suffering, the Enemy's favorite weapon in defeating us, depressing us, and holding us back from the love we were created to receive.

Shame[1] is always being leveraged by the Enemy to tell a story where you end up alone. Our discomfort with expressing the honest, sad truth of our experience reveals a deeper truth about the storyline steering our lives. The shame born in the garden silently stalks us today, trying to convince us no one cares, nothing can improve, and expressing weakness will only further isolate us instead of connecting us to hope. We have to acknowledge shame's presence to inhabit the embodied story of sight, to step toward the communion we were made for.

Shame, as psychiatrist Curt Thompson so powerfully describes, is the primary tool evil uses to disrupt and disconnect our relationships, our stories, our communities, and our world.[2] It is the felt sense that I am bad, there really is something wrong with me, and I don't matter to anyone else.[3] Shame is the stealthy, compelling energy evil is constantly using to distract us from living in the story where grace is here.

1   Not all shame is inherently bad. It's a biological response meant to protect us from harm and abandonment. Even so, evil uses it to powerfully disrupt our ability to be grounded in the love of God and other humans. In his book *The Pandora Problem*, E. James Wilder makes a helpful distinction between relational shame and toxic shame. Relationships require shame to maintain health, and we each need to foster the skill of giving and receiving healthy shame messages to acknowledge the truth of how we are living alongside the hope of where we are headed. E. James Wilder, *The Pandora Problem: Facing Narcissism in Leaders and Ourselves* (Carmel, IN: Deeper Walk International, 2018).

2   Curt Thompson, *The Soul of Shame* (Downers Grove, IL: InterVarsity Press, 2015), 24.

3   Brené Brown, *I Thought It Was Just Me (But It Isn't): Making the Journey from "What Will People Think?" to "I Am Enough"* (New York: Gotham, 2008), 13.

Before we even have words to acknowledge or ascribe meaning to its disturbing presence, shame is felt in our bodies in the dynamic interplay of relationship. It arises from condescending or mean words, sure, but it also ignites in the million ways we sense another person might not care or might be judging us. Before we consciously register we've noticed, our bodies are responding to the nonverbal cues of others. Shame starts with the sigh of someone who is tired of listening to us, an irritated glance, or lack of eye contact in a conversation. The dam of shame has often been released before we realize it, starting from the lower regions of our brains.

Shame quickly and powerfully disrupts the integration of the lower and upper regions of our brains, biologically isolating parts of ourselves from one another. We become overwhelmed by the current of energy in our brain stems and temporarily unable to access the regulating, rational functions of the upper region of our brains, the prefrontal cortex.[4] Without thinking, we turn our gaze away from others to deal with the rush of painful emotion, but turning away only reinforces the sense that we are alone and that we have to deal with this, and everything, on our own. Shame paralyzes us and blocks us from hope, because it tells the untrue story that we are the only ones who can get ourselves out of the mess we are in. It's the neurobiological process behind our prideful self-sufficiency, the instinct pushing us to chew our sorrows into stories of success.

Psychiatrist and trauma expert Judith Lewis Herman describes shame as "a relatively wordless state, in which speech and thought are inhibited."[5] She elaborates, "It is also an acutely self-conscious state; the person feels small, ridiculous, and exposed. There is a wish to hide, characteristically expressed by covering the face with

4   Thompson, *The Soul of Shame*, 67.
5   Judith Lewis Herman, "Shattered Shame States and Their Repair," in *Shattered States: Disorganised Attachment and Its Repair*, ed. Judy Yellen and Kate White (London: Karnac, 2012), 160–61.

the hands. . . . Shame is always implicitly a relational experience."[6]
Our faces flush. We look down and away. We feel worthless, confused, and scared.

Shame hijacks us, persuading us, often without our awareness,
to live according to our culture's story of self-sufficient hiding and
pretending. It is the emotional sense "that I do not have what it takes
to tolerate this moment or circumstance."[7] As such, shame word-
lessly tells our bodies the story that we are abandoned, unlovable,
and headed for harm. It convinces us to disconnect, self-protect,
and detach from where we are and who we are.

⚓

In early 2015 I had to get all new doctors after joining my husband's
work insurance plan. I'm part of the unfortunate 20 percent or so
of ankylosing spondylitis (AS) patients whose bloodwork is nearly
always normal, making my body more of a puzzle than a provable
artifact of disease. My previous rheumatologist was a short, red-
haired woman whose spark matched her kindness. She always took
time to listen during our appointments and seriously considered
my exceedingly extensive family history[8] in treating my enigmatic
symptoms with respect. Before her, my experience with rheumatol-
ogists included both doctors who cared and listened and those who
treated me like an inconvenience, or worse, a liar. Her kindness had
given me hope that the days of needing to prove myself to doctors
were over.

....
6   Ibid.
7   Thompson, *The Soul of Shame*, 25.
8   My older brother and younger sister both have autoimmune diseases, along
with a wild number of others strewn throughout both sides of our family tree.
One time my sister's doctor actually told us, "So, basically, your family has pretty
f'd-up genes." Usually when I share my family history with a new doctor, they look
dumbfounded and say something like, "Wow. I've never seen a history quite like this
before." It's super fun.

I entered the tiny exam room of my new rheumatologist's office ready to give a full personal and family history. And I came alone. I'm a professional patient. Strong. Capable of advocating for myself. I figured at six years into being sick, I could handle the visit on my own. Why make my husband use a personal day?

From the moment the tall, blond doctor strode into the room, something was off. He didn't shake my hand or look me in the eye but instead went directly to the computer to read from my chart, where his gaze remained for the next two minutes. When he finally turned around, he gave me no invitation to share my history but instead unequivocally stated he believed I was a case of misdiagnosis and malpractice.

Without hearing my voice or touching my body, he reduced six years of treatment to a mistake. In his eyes I was a blight of the medical system, wrongly passed from one doctor to another without proof to warrant the extreme measures that had been taken to treat my pain and keep me functioning. Before five minutes had passed, my worst nightmare was becoming a reality.

I was face to face with the person who had the power to ensure I would continue receiving the care that kept me out of bed, and he was unwilling to give it. Without hearing my story, without knowing the way my body had so dramatically responded to treatment over the years, without listening to the ways disease had split through my life like an ax, this towering, self-assured doctor had dismissed the reality that had taken all of my strength to survive.

Though I cannot remember the full course of our conversation, probably because the experience was more painful than my mind could bear, I do remember feeling the expanse of my fate spread before me like a charcoal cloud. Desperate to push away the future I most feared, I tried using my clearest words in my most determined, respectable tone. My attempt to be heard only amplified his aggression. Six years of doctors' appointments and a lifetime of fortifying myself against waves of harm gave me the courage to say no to being treated with contempt by a person under oath to do no harm.

I pressed hard into the handles of the chair, toughening my resolve, and looked straight into the eyes of the man who didn't have the respect to look into mine.

"Who is your superior?" I asked. "Who can I see for a second opinion? I am not willing to have you be my doctor."

More condescension ensued, but the scales of power had subtly shifted.

Yet even in my strength, my soul trembled at the possibility that this was it—the future I feared, the black unraveling of days in which I would only get sicker because no one would see or care enough to help. I wasn't sure I could survive that future.

Shame was the blade cutting apart my calm and hope in that exam room, not because I felt stupid or bad but because I felt unable to tolerate the terror of the moment. I was in the presence of someone who was supposed to care and help, but met with judgment. I felt terrified and alone. Shame was forecasting the coming chapter of my life as one of sickness eliciting suspicion, pain with no relief, suffering with only myself to rely on for help. I left angry and anxious but, especially, I left with less hope.

Shame was telling a scary story about my life, the same story it tries to tell me in times of distress now. Shame whispers the taunting story of defeat and diminishment in our moments of stress. It cuts against our hope and fuels our fear in suffering, even if we don't think it's the main problem we face, even if it's not the reason you picked up this book on suffering.

Maybe the pervading feeling you have is anxiety about your suffering. You fear how you'll pay for therapy, doctors' appointments, or the divorce lawyer, but really, isn't that fear about not having enough for the situation you find yourself in? Maybe you fear having to tell your small group at church about your marriage problems or how sad you really feel about still being single, but isn't that fear about feeling you won't be able to tolerate how uncomfortable telling them might be? You anticipate being judged or not really being heard, and that anticipation is shame expressed in anxiety. We fear being diminished by the suffering in our lives, becoming less human, less okay, less in control of stopping our lives from becoming a dark descent into a terrible future.

Shame wants us to believe the story that weakness is a private, avoidable problem we should overcome by ourselves. When everything around us treats weakness like a personal problem to master, when we suffer and it does not cease, shame becomes more palpable. When your disease isn't healed, your marriage doesn't last, or your mental health is lacking, you have to both experience weakness and cope with it in a world that tells you it is your fault.

Evil uses shaming encounters like the one I experienced with that doctor to shrink our expectations of the grace we can receive in relationships. It reinforces the story that we will be judged, unheard, and stuck. Evil uses shame to isolate us so thoroughly that we become trapped in a cycle of expecting judgment and prejudging most people as unwilling or unable to hear, help, and love. The people who could remind us of hope are viewed as probable enemies. We fear being honest will just make us hurt worse. We silence ourselves in shame, withholding truth about suffering, because of the unspoken, preemptive verdict that grace won't be here.

Shame tells the story that we are alone and must make our own way through the distress we feel. It diminishes us in suffering by coaxing us to ignore the pain, minimize it, and pretend everything is more okay than it is. It's sin, energized, silently persuading us to stay in hiding. Shame wants us to live divided, dishonest, disembodied lives, to treat our bodies and stories like failures to conceal, to let our lips say we believe God is good while our hearts stay discouraged in the dark. The most harrowing power of shame might be its stealth in convincing us that silencing our pain behind statements of God's goodness is spiritual, when really it's just a churchy form of self-sufficiency.

It is only in honesty and exposure, in being seen in our sadness and despair, that we'll most clearly see the truth that we're still living in a story of love.

⚓

The scariest part of being human might be the moments of exposure, when others see how deeply we need to be held. Every human bears the scar of our first relational severing, the disconnection from God we inherited from Adam and Eve's choice to seek self-sufficiency, to be more godlike than their bodies could hold. Our bodies bear the memory of our perceived abandonment from God. At the slightest hint of rejection or the ringing impression of danger, our bodies instinctively respond with shame's self-protection. We turn our gaze from those who could hurt us. Adrenaline, noradrenaline, and cortisol rush without our conscious consent, readying us to fight or flee the vulnerability of exposure.

But down to the fiber of our muscles and the double-helix cascade that carries the stories and traumas and hopes of our every ancestor, our bodies also bear the memory of unsevered love.

Not that long ago, there was a season when I couldn't even feel sadness for myself anymore. A lifetime of hurt and a recent string of horrible circumstances had left me depressed and disconnected. I can usually keep at least one finger on grace, but I'd entirely lost my grip. I couldn't see a way out of my colossal, consuming pain. Out of the financial burden of surviving illness. Out of the defeat of being harmed by the body of Christ caring more about image than people. Out of the agony of living in a body mired by abuse and disease.

My hands couldn't touch grace. They only held the sharp edges of a shattered life, fingers wrapped in a bloodied fist shaking at the God who kept letting shards of brokenness fall from the sky.

The only grace I saw was the alluring idea of forcing handfuls of pills down my throat to end the terror of what God had allowed my life to become. I'm a therapist who knows all the right responses to suicidal ideation, and my heart throbbed with the quick pulse of shamefully considering what I counsel so many others to reject.

My husband found me staring blankly at the bedroom wall, pills on my bedside table, contemplating despair. He sat at my feet, placing his hands on my legs, meeting my stony face with a look of concern, care, and fear.

"What's wrong?"

I fidgeted, focusing on a paper clip on my lap, twisting it into the uselessness I felt faith was. I stared at my hands, at the table, at the wall, anywhere but the two eyes, glassy with tears, staring back at the emptiness I wanted to maintain.

"I'm . . . I don't think I want to be alive anymore."

My eyes came to Ryan's for a moment, a flicker of hope followed by a flash of fear. I had revealed myself to him, sharing the terrible truth of the darkness underneath my hollow expression.

I was exposed.

My body trembled with the terror of speaking my faithlessness out loud. In the silence, I grabbed the pillow next to me, burying my face and its shame.

Ryan touched my shoulder, turned my chin from the pillow, and held my face in his two warm hands, breaking my attention from the furious flood of shame that had swamped me in the elapsed silence of four seconds.

"I love you."

I met his eyes for a moment, his words and hands startling me out of my silent wake.

"I'm so sorry you are hurting so much. I hate this for you."

I looked up, disbelief disarmed. Ryan wasn't ashamed of my shame. He wasn't afraid of my faithlessness. I glanced at my hands, at my chest, searching my body for proof that I was worthy of acceptance. I found it in his face.

In that moment, I didn't need someone to tell me God was still good. I needed someone to show me I was still loved—even when drowning in the violent storm of shame. Exposing my need was a grace that allowed another's empathy to surprise me with hope.

When we allow someone who is empathetic and safe to see our pain, shame, and need, we place our bodies in a position to remember original love. Written into our brains' basic way of responding to each other is an exchange that can form hope where we feel only despair. While I sank in my shame, Ryan's presence of love and acceptance began to change the story I was believing about my present and future. My brain's mirror neuron system responded to Ryan's display of love.[9] Our bodies throb with the longing for love and intuitively absorb its presence. A lifetime of grief, dismissal, and suffering had diminished my brain's capacity to feel loved, valuable, and safe in my present suffering, but seeing someone extend empathy reignited the neural pathways that could generate my hope and healing.

Suffering can wring the will to live right out of us, until all that is left is a desperate drop. If you have felt hopeless, if despair has darkened your ability to see light, please know you are not alone. Losing the will to live can be a natural consequence of being human in a life battered by suffering. To feel this way is more common than you might think. And you are more valuable than shame wants you to believe. Let your hopelessness be heard. Be honest and specific— with yourself and others—about just how dark your thoughts have become.[10] If you feel anywhere near how I felt in this story, please

....
9   Giacomo Rizzolatti and Laila Craighero, "The Mirror-Neuron System," *Annual Review of Neuroscience* 27 (2004): 169–92.
10 I wish more Christians knew that suicide is not the result of a lack of faith or a

honor the gravity of what you've endured by seeking professional help from a licensed counselor or therapist. We won't judge you.

Whether you have felt suicidal or not, hear the truth I've learned again and again. Most of us fear the exposure of our wounds and deepest faithlessness will separate us from love, but exposure is the substance of our healing. The nakedness of suffering leads us to the embodied experience of receiving God's clothing of love.

Finding grace in suffering is less about cognitively assenting to the truth of God's goodness than about letting our shame be seen. If you are a sufferer, be seen. If you encounter someone's suffering, tuck your words of God's goodness away until you've first listened with the eyes of your heart determined to not look away from pain.

It's the shared sight and sound of what we usually keep hidden that carries our bodies into stories larger than shame.

Shame is constantly trying to shape the story we tell about our suffering. It is always countering the narrative of God's nearness with the story that we are unloved, abandoned, and will forever be stuck in a place of pain.

Like Adam and Eve, we sew together fig leaves for ourselves to cover the pain and shame of suffering. We hide, blame, rationalize, and overspiritualize, trying to think our way into comfort to make sense of the evil we experience. But God provides himself.

There is a bigger, truer story than shame, striving, and hiding.

Suffering makes us want to hide, but God pursues us in our naked shame so we can be known and clothed. When Adam and

---

lack of truth. Suicide results from complex pain in broken bodies aching for redemption. We remain a people of hope when we are honest about hopelessness. If you are feeling hopeless, please share with someone. If you can't bring yourself to share with someone you know or don't have anyone to call right now, you can always call the National Suicide Prevention Hotline anytime, day or night, at 1-800-273-8255. You are worth every awkward, hard conversation. Your life matters.

Eve deflected God's healing pursuit after their sin, he pursued them and provided for them anyway, clothing them in animal skins to cover their vulnerable bodies outside the safety of the garden.[11] Later God provided the lasting clothing for our shame, the righteousness of his Son, who came to live in a fragile body like Adam's and Eve's, like yours and mine, in a world where shame appears to hold the power over the possibility of what our lives could become.

We often feel crushed by the weight of our suffering—with no other response possible but to hide or give up or pretend we believe—because we forget our pain started in a story bigger than personal failure or inadequacy. We see our days descending into a darkness we fear, and we don't remember our lives are woven into a story larger than the sum of twenty or eighty years.

Your life is part of a story larger than your own, but if you do not hear and remember and tell the bigger story, you'll stay confused, lost, and weary. When you only see the pain of your past and present, you are wandering without the map to your future joy and future home. You're a desert in a drought, crumbling and cracked and in need of the rain of reminding and remembrance.

There is a love that transcends time. There is a story larger than the reality you see.

To find our way through the shame of suffering, we must look to another's shame lifted up. We must remember the story where pain was born in sin, shame came from a serpent, and God came to find us.

There is a story that transcends our suffering by entering into it.

The gospel is good news for sufferers, not only because it makes joy in suffering possible but also because it creates and demonstrates our joy through God's great grace of entering a body that would groan, cry, and die. The gospel establishes a pattern of incarnation as the right response to suffering. Instead of dropping a

....
11 Gen. 3:21.

word of truth, we should be compelled by the gospel to stand in each other's suffering, in bodies displaying God's truth, in our willingness to be honest about darkness, death, and the defeat we feel.

A larger story encompasses our stories of suffering. To inhabit and experience the story that is far better than self-sufficiency, we have to learn how to tell the time in light of where Scripture says we exist in the bigger story of God's love.[12] It's not just Thursday; it's Thursday in redemptive history, in a story where Jesus came but has not yet returned.

God entered the human story in the body of his beloved Son to provide the clothing for our shame we could never sew with our grasping, fragile hands. He doesn't turn away from our shame; he pursues us in it with loving sight and his own body. In John 19, we read that when Jesus was crucified, the soldiers stripped him, took his clothing, and divided it among themselves by casting lots. They put him to open shame. Jesus hung on a cross—naked and exposed—so you and I could be clothed in his love.

We lose hope in navigating our stories of suffering because we need to know, feel, and experience the story that God has drawn near. This is the context of the unfolding story of this book and the unfolding story of your suffering: God has drawn near in the presence of his Son and his people and has provided the clothing you need to be whole. Where we attempt to cover our own shame, Jesus became shame for us.

....
12 I am not sure where I first came across the concept of "telling the time," of remembering where we are as saints in redemptive history as a central means of knowing how our stories are part of God's larger story. I think it was probably while studying at Covenant College, perhaps under Dr. Kelly Kapic. Bryant Myers also refers to our need to "know what time it is." Bryant L. Myers, *Walking with the Poor: Principles and Practices of Transformational Development* (Maryknoll, NY: Orbis, 2009), 21.

One day Jesus will return with power to reclaim all that feels lost to shame and suffering. His warm, wounded hands will hold our downcast faces, looking us in the eyes with respect for the pain we've endured; and with the utmost gentleness, he'll wipe every tear from our eyes. Death, grief, crying, and pain will be done.[13] God will return to live with us forever.

Here in the space between Jesus' resurrection and our final tears, we have to remember the time we are at in the story. Shame will try again and again to disorient and disconnect us from the hope God has provided, but its defeat is certain. When we remember to tell the time, we remember our individual stories are part of the larger story of humanity broken, beloved, and redeemed. We have not been left alone in our suffering. Rather, we've been pursued by the God who made us, clothed by his own experience of shame, and invited to be known in the weakness we most fear.

Here in our hurry and hiding, we are invited to the grace of being known. The wounds of suffering require dressing we can't apply or change on our own. The story of love can't be lived with spoken truth but hidden hurt. God is moving us from hiding to honest, from naked to clothed, from ashamed and alone in singular stories to attached and amazed in a shared story of his solidarity with suffering and his unending commitment to redeem us in love.

....
13 Rev. 21:4.

CHAPTER 3

TRIUNE LOVE

You Were Made for Relationship

> *To say that I am made in the image of God is to say*
> *that love is the reason for my existence, for God is*
> *love. Love is my true identity. . . . Love is my true*
> *character. Love is my name.*

—THOMAS MERTON, *NEW SEEDS OF CONTEMPLATION*

I'm hiking to a waterfall with friends, glancing at yellow trail markers on trees as I soak in the scent of ponderosa pines and marvel at the sight of their towering splendor. Light pours through the heavy canopy of branches above like small streams of heaven into the darkness of the thick forest. I'm nowhere more alive than with my feet on the spongy softness of pine needles, my eyes dancing in the glory of green, and my fingers pointing out the tiny theophanies of small, wild things.[1] The mountain bluebird's shy song joins the sparrow's ringing refrain, their melodies merging in a chorus of joy. I smile in the freedom of creatures who sing,

....
1   Tish Harrison Warren uses the lovely phrase "tiny theophanies" in her book *Liturgy of the Ordinary: Sacred Practices in Everyday Life* (Downers Grove, IL: InterVarsity Press, 2016), 135.

sustained and fed by God. My mind lights with Jesus' reminder to "consider the birds of the sky: They don't sow or reap or gather into barns, yet your heavenly Father feeds them. Aren't you worth more than they?"[2]

As I turn my daydreaming mind from the bird-filled trees back to the trail, though, I no longer see my friends.

I call out, but no one answers.

Where can they be?

My heart beats faster as I turn my head from side to side, searching the forest for faces.

Maybe they kept going without me, since I walk a little more slowly than they do. Sometimes my arthritic gait slows me down.

I keep walking, trying to calm my pounding heart, hoping I'll find my friends around the next turn in the trail, laughing and calling for me to catch up.

I reach the next bend and the next, and they are still nowhere in sight. The sparse forest light that was enchanting now seems threatening. It's dark out here, and eerily quiet. I stop walking to listen for noises of people, but all I hear are the birds, which frankly are now the farthest thing from beautiful or encouraging. I'm alone, and unlike the birds, I am not built to survive by foraging, thank you very much.

I keep walking for a few minutes, but the trail is blocked by a large fallen log, moist and decaying in the damp air. I try to cross it, but it's too big. I can't get my legs up high enough to straddle its heft. My arms are too weak to hoist myself up. I shove branches aside, looking for a way around the impasse. Thorns scratch my hands and arms, and branches snap against my face, as I struggle through the thickness with fury and alarm. *Why couldn't they just wait for me?*

....
2   Matt. 6:26.

I've found a way around the log, but in my slight detour I've lost the trail entirely.

Where are they?

I scream. I yell. I start to cry.

I'm alone in a place I usually love, and I'm not sure which way to go in the haunting amber glow of sunset that is pulling the little light left into a dark, cavernous night.

This is how suffering can feel.

Suffering is like a forest whose light is threatening, a place we lose our companions. We panic as we wonder if we will ever find a way out. When suffering invades our lives, we feel lost, left behind by the church while they keep blissfully hiking toward a waterfall of grace we fear we'll never reach.

The thing is, we aren't the only ones who are lost.

Without a theology of suffering rooted in a relational understanding of personhood, the whole church loses her way to her true hope and home. The church has swallowed self-sufficiency as the goal of living, and in doing so, she struggles to nourish saints with the food of communion. The church puts herself in a wilderness by allowing her life to be guided more by the storylines of individualism and shame than the story of communion. In this wilderness, we're unable to hear each other's cries for help. We stare admiringly at solitary pine trees, pondering their longevity and assuming that strong, faithful lives grow in the soil of our individual determination to be rooted in biblical truth.

When we do not have a theology of suffering rooted in communion, we are left with platitudes, empty promises, and people wandering instead of wonder-ing. We become lost in the forest of unexamined individualism, hiking toward a waterfall that will never satisfy eyes made to dance and glow in the glory of communion.

We are all lost. Rediscovering the goal of our personhood rooted in the inner life of God as Father, Son, and Holy Spirit is where we will be found.

What the weary and broken and secretly apathetic and pious alike need today is not more prodding to believe God is good. From cradle Christians to those flirting with entering the church's front door, from the poorest to the richest, from the cynic to the pastor, we all need to be captivated by a love greater than our guilt. We need to be captured by the story where individual effort melts in a rushing river of shared grace. We need water that flows when we are fragile, grace that girds when we are weak, hope that holds us when our hands are empty, holiness that hears and shatters our pride, and a faith far deeper and more mysterious than a mere affirmation that God is good. We need to be pulled into God's goodness in embodied experiences reflecting who he is.

"What we need today," Scottish theologian James Torrance writes, "is a better understanding of the person not just as an individual but as someone who finds his or her true being-in-communion with God and with others, the counterpart of a Trinitarian doctrine of God."[3] The church desperately needs a revised anthropology, a fuller vision of ourselves as embodied and relational and our stories as beautifully, inextricably bound together in a larger story of love.

To find our way through suffering, we must trace the contours of how God made us *for* relationships in bodies shaped *by* relationships. After God made sky and earth out of formless emptiness, spoke light into being, and channeled water and dust into sea and soil, before birds and trees had names, he said, "Let us make man in our image, according to our likeness."[4] God stooped to the dirt

....
3   James B. Torrance, "The Doctrine of the Trinity in Our Contemporary Situation," in *The Forgotten Trinity: A Selection of Papers Presented to the BCC Study Commission on Trinitarian Doctrine Today,* ed. Alasdair I. C. Heron (London: British Council of Churches, 1991), 15.
4   Gen. 1:26.

of his brand-new world and breathed us into being to reflect his relational likeness. We were made to reflect the "us" and "our" of the God who created all things by the power of his voice and breath.

As Father, Son, and Holy Spirit, God is a community of love—one God yet three particular persons relating to each other in perfect unity. The best summative description Scripture gives of God is love. John tells us in 1 John 4:16, "We have come to know and to believe the love that God has for us. *God is love,* and the one who remains in love remains in God, and God remains in him" (emphasis added).

God's inner nature and activity of love reveal the most fundamental ground and goal of our existence. The triune God is the reality in which "we live and move and have our being."[5] Dallas Willard's words help us imagine the goodness of the Trinity's constant communion: "Think of the most vibrant personal company that you can imagine, and multiply that by a factor of infinity, and you have begun to get a glimpse of what God is doing, where he is, what he was doing before the foundation of the earth, and what he will be doing forever. That is the being upon whom a life without lack relies. Such a life is guaranteed for those whose minds are set upon this God in faith."[6]

This is our end—sharing in God's absolute, eternal delight.[7]

We were created as an overflow of the eternal joy existing between Father, Son, and Spirit in their perfect love for one another. Our existence is pure gift and generosity, springing from love rather than need. As my mentor, systematic theologian Kelly Kapic, writes, "The God who did not need to create, who is eternally complete in

----

5   Acts 17:28.

6   Dallas Willard, *Life without Lack: Living in the Fullness of Psalm 23* (Nashville: Nelson, 2018), 19.

7   As theologian Alan Torrance writes, "The communion of the Trinity as such constitutes the *arche* and *telos* of all that is." Alan J. Torrance, *Persons in Communion: An Essay on Trinitarian Description and Human Participation, with Special Reference to Volume One of Karl Barth's Church Dogmatics* (Edinburgh: T&T Clark, 2011), 258.

himself, is the God who *does* create, who continues to uphold what he created, and who takes a personal interest in each life and molecule of creation."[8] That we embodied breaths of dust[9] even exist is a wonder beyond our comprehension. Love created us, sustains us, and invites us into his joy.

We were made in the image of the God who is relationship. The image of God is not simply in you and in me. It is in *us*. The reflection of God's well of inner love is most visible in how you and I relate to one another; his light of love is refracted and its color formed in our shared presence.[10] The breath of God enlivening our dust into love is most visible in the space shared between us. We most reflect God not simply in our individuality but in our interdependence.

Being made in the image of the God who is love means being made for relationship.[11] The goal of living as a person created to reflect, radiate, and receive love can never be self-sufficiency. It has to be communion.

....

8   Kelly M. Kapic, *God So Loved, He Gave* (Grand Rapids: Zondervan, 2010), 18.

9   In *The City of God*, Augustine describes humans as *terra animata*, animated earth. Rather than reifying the mind, rationality, or even self-awareness, Augustine highlighted God's breath as the animating power turning what was previously mere dust and dirt into the glory of animated physicality reflecting God's own image. Stephen Sapp articulates the importance of this embodied anthropology in how we view one another when disease or disorders minimize our rational capabilities, insights which carry great import for viewing and treating those who suffer as whole, beautiful reflections of God. Drawing from Augustinian insights, Gilbert Meilaender likewise challenges us, especially as it pertains to bioethics, to hold with humility and wonder the natural progression of death. See St. Augustine, *De Civitate Dei*, trans. Henry Bettenson (New York: Penguin Books, 1972), 20. See also Stephen Sapp, "Living with Alzheimer's: Body, Soul and the Remembering Community," *Christian Century* 115, no. 2 (1998): 54–60. And Gilbert Meilaender, "Terra es Animata: On Having a Life," *Hastings Center Report* 23, no. 4 (1993): 25–32.

10 Stanley J. Grenz, *The Social God and the Relational Self: A Trinitarian Theology of the Imago Dei*, vol. 1 (Louisville: Westminster John Knox, 2001), 305.

11 Theologian Colin Gunton writes, "To be human is to be created in and for relationship with divine and human others." Colin E. Gunton, *The One, the Three and the Many* (New York: Cambridge Univ. Press, 1993), 222.

As psychology professor John A. Teske writes, ". . . we are ourselves only in communion. What we are *about* is outside ourselves, is *other*. What we *are*, even as our individual selves are not internal spaces, connected to each other, but literally, and externally, composed of each other. We redeem each other *bodily*."[12] We become most human, the radiant reflections of God, through relationship.[13] Communion is the substance, sustenance, and resolution of humanity, the invitation to share in the eternal joy of God. It happens—we become most fully human—through interdependence. We most reflect and radiate our glorious God not when we are standing strong, tall, and self-sustained but when we hold each other up in respect and self-giving love.

Being human is about living in relationships that affirm and contribute to our uniqueness and unity, relationships that empower through self-giving, relationships where dignity and individuality are upheld and nurtured, relationships where we encounter one another with reverence. Theologian Serene Jones affirms this, writing, "God created me among us, me inseparable from us, me for us and them for me."[14] When we relate to one another with sacred attention, we step into the light of who God is. God's inner life of love is reflected

....

12 John A. Teske, "From Embodied to Extended Cognition," *Zygon* 48 (2013): 759–87, doi:10.1111/zygo.12038.

13 Orthodox theologian John Zizioulas writes, "The Person is otherness in communion and communion in otherness. The person is an identity that emerges through relationship . . . ; it is an 'I' that can exist only as long as it relates to a 'thou' which affirms its existence and its otherness. If we isolate the 'I' from the 'thou' we lose not only its otherness but also its very being; it simply cannot be without the other. This is what distinguishes the person from an individual. The orthodox understanding of the holy Trinity is the only way to arrive at this notion of personhood." John D. Zizioulas, *Communion and Otherness: Further Studies in Personhood and the Church* (New York: T&T Clark, 2006), 9.

14 Serene Jones, *Call It Grace: Finding Meaning in a Fractured World* (New York: Viking, 2019), 152.

in our gazes and glances, our words and shared silences, our prayers, tears, and sight, our long hugs in the terrors of the night.

We were made for communion, and our bodies, brains, and even the most primal patterns of human development show relationships are the center of our existence. From conception to death, we cannot survive or sufficiently develop outside of relationship. Who we are, both in our understanding of our identity and in our ability to regulate the basic functions of living with hearts that beat and lungs that breathe, comes into being only through relationship.

Every human is born into the vulnerability of dependence; our experience with one another forms the structure of our brains and the possibility of our thriving.[15] We are born with an innate longing and need for connection, demonstrated in the formation and energetic flow of our infant brains to attach to our parents or primary caregivers.[16] We were created to form a secure sense of self and worth in the matrix of eye contact and being heard, held, and soothed. Our earliest moments and months form the foundation of a lifetime of being able to trust and love both humans and God. Our relational experiences shape our mind's capacity to experience God as trustworthy, loving, and present—or not.

No one describes the process of attachment more beautifully than psychologist Henry Cloud.

> If everything goes right we begin to bond naturally as infants. When we are born we move from a warm, wet, dark, soothing environment into a cold, dry, bright, harsh one. We move from our mother's womb, where all our needs are automatically met, to a world where we need to depend upon fallible people to take

....
15 Daniel J. Siegel and Tina Payne Bryson, *The Whole-Brain Child: 12 Revolutionary Strategies to Nurture Your Child's Developing Mind* (New York: Bantam, 2012), 7.
16 Daniel J. Siegel, *The Developing Mind: How Relationships and the Brain Interact to Shape Who We Are* (New York: Guilford, 2012), chap. 3.

care of us. For those few moments after we slip from the birth canal into the light, we are in shock, in emotional isolation.

One look at the face of a newborn gives you a good picture of this total isolation. Then the mother takes the child and begins to hold him closely and talk softly to him. Suddenly he goes through a transformation. He stops screaming, and his muscles relax. He turns toward his mother for warmth, for food, and for love. Emotional bonding to his mother has begun.

Over time the child gradually internalizes his mother's care. He begins storing up memories of being comforted by her. In a sense, the child takes his mother in and stores her inside his memory. This internalization gives him a greater and greater sense of security. He has a storehouse of loving memories upon which to draw in his mother's absence.

A "self-soothing" system is being formed in which the child can literally have a relationship with the one who loves him in her absence. He could not do this immediately because he did not have enough loving experiences. Through thousands of moments of connection the memory traces must be built up.

As this relationship gets stronger and stronger, the child reaches another milestone: he achieves "emotional object constancy." What this means is that the child is able to experience himself as loved constantly, even in the absence of the loved one. And he also is able to love the absent one, whom he has internalized.[17]

God made us permeable.[18] We are like sponges, soaking up the relational atmosphere around us. And we are most spongy in our first two to three years of life, as our brains "borrow" our

....

17 Henry Cloud, *Changes That Heal: How to Understand Your Past to Ensure a Healthier Future* (Grand Rapids: Zondervan, 2009), 68–69.
18 Rich Plass and Jim Cofield, *The Relational Soul* (Downers Grove, IL: InterVarsity Press, 2014), 25.

parents' brains, particularly their prefrontal cortices, to organize and regulate our own functioning.[19] Our brains form and function through absorbing our parents' presence. We internalize our relationship with our parents or earliest caregivers, whether that relationship was adequate, abusive, confusing, or wonderful. Their presence shaped the physiologic structure of our brains and the capacity of our hearts to trust and love. Even when we are adults, our lives are guided by the relational atmosphere we absorb, forming us toward faith or doubt.

We were made for relationships in bodies shaped by relationships. Remembering this changes how we find grace in suffering and how we all can find wholeness in the stories God is writing in our lives. Remember, we are more than walking heads.[20] We are embodied and relational, walking, eating, talking, hugging, touching, sitting reflections of the God who is three in one and showed his face in Jesus.

"Somehow we Christians have come to believe that we *have* bodies, not that we *are* bodies."[21] We elevate our thinking capacity over the truth of our embodied, relational existence, and in doing so, we cut ourselves off from the grace of learning love through one another. God wants to renew our minds so we know his good, pleasing, and perfect will, and he renews them through us presenting our bodies as living sacrifices.[22] Faith is formation for our whole selves. Hope is held in physical, relational experiences.

....
19 Lois Cozolino, *The Neuroscience of Human Relationships: Attachment and the Developing Social Brain* (New York: Norton, 2014), 83. See also John H. Coe and Todd W. Hall, *Psychology in the Spirit: Contours of a Transformational Psychology* (Downers Grove, IL: InterVarsity Press, 2010), 241.
20 Brad D. Strawn and Warren S. Brown, "Liturgical Animals: What Psychology and Neuroscience Tell Us about Formation and Worship," *Liturgy* 28, no. 4 (2013): 3.
21 Warren S. Brown and Brad D. Strawn, *The Physical Nature of Christian Life: Neuroscience, Psychology, and the Church* (New York: Cambridge Univ. Press, 2012), 4.
22 Rom. 12:1-2.

Throughout this book, I will discuss the brain and the beautiful ways neuroscience reflects the transformative nature of relationships in the body of Christ. The brain is more than a three-pound mass at the top of our bodies, buzzing with more than 86 billion neurons.[23] As psychiatrist Dan Siegel, a pioneer in the field of interpersonal neurobiology,[24] reminds us, "The mind is embodied, not just enskulled."[25]

Your mind involves your whole body, including the activity of the brain throughout the body.[26] It extends beyond your gray matter. Through both the synapses firing inside your skull and the brain's distributed nervous system throughout your body, the mind connects with the world both within and beyond your skin. The mind depends on the presence of relationships to share energy and information and is both structured and changed by relationships. It regulates how energy flows through us, guiding the communication of neurons and creating the perceptions, sensations, emotions, beliefs, and meaning filling our lives in every moment.[27] Your embodied, relational mind is what God is renewing.

How we come to believe, trust, and love is a physical process. Being rooted and grounded in love requires relationships to guide our embodied, relational minds to renewed faith in the God who

....

23 Eric H. Chudler, "Brain Facts That Make You Go, 'Hmmmmm,'" University of Washington (n.d.), *https://faculty.washington.edu/chudler/ffacts.html* (accessed July 5, 2019).

24 Interpersonal neurobiology (IPNB) is an interdisciplinary field that brings together many branches of science and theories of human knowledge and meaning. It is a major influence on my therapeutic work and is a body of knowledge that has significantly contributed to my thinking in this book. IPNB beautifully expresses what Scripture has always stated, that our personhood is formed, expressed, and sustained by relationships.

25 Siegel, *The Developing Mind,* 5.

26 Curt Thompson, *The Soul of Shame: Retelling the Stories We Believe about Ourselves* (Downers Grove, IL: InterVarsity Press, 2015), 39.

27 Daniel J. Siegel, *Mindsight: The New Science of Personal Transformation* (New York: Bantam, 2011), 54–55.

is good. Relationships are required, not peripheral. We are to let the word of Christ dwell richly among us, in the context of our communal life together.[28] As Siegel explains, "The brain is a social organ, and our relationships with one another are not a luxury but an essential nutrient for our survival."[29]

Our relationships shape the story we live, not just the one we speak with our lips but the one we feel in our bones and believe when we're most broken. Relationships have shaped our minds, constructing the way we experience our stories, tell them, and participate in God's story. When we prod each other to believe God is working all things together for our good, we miss the larger grace we could extend in re-forming our mind's potential to experience him as trustworthy and present. Our struggle to believe, our striving to succeed, our prideful, solo journeys to look stronger, more competent, and more put together than we are—all are rooted in relational experiences of feeling overlooked, neglected, insignificant, and small.

We see God through our scars.

To see God clearly, to believe with heart and soul and mind and strength, we have to see our wounds and let them be dressed. We can't just consume theological facts about God and expect them to digest into a nourished, vibrant faith.[30] If God seems absent, it may be because you've experienced an absence in your life so deep and so incompletely healed you wince anytime it's brushed against. If God seems against you, perhaps it's because people who should have been for you treated you with contempt or neglect.

....

28 Col. 3:12–17. While embodied relationships are the normal way in which God works, God can and does sustain his children outside the scope of the relational interaction I'm describing, when no positive relationships are available or possible. But this is the exception, not the rule.

29 Siegel, *Mindsight*, 211.

30 Curt Thompson, *Anatomy of the Soul: Surprising Connections between Neuroscience and Spiritual Practices That Can Transform Your Life and Relationships* (Carol Stream, IL: Tyndale, 2010), 133.

We were made for union with God, but we came into being through relationships fractured by sin. Your concept of God has been formed synapse by synapse in your earliest experiences, in your memories of harm and help, and the overall presence you internalized from your parents. Your struggle to experience God as good and present almost certainly has less to do with your doctrinal beliefs and memorized Scripture than with the way you've been shaped and scarred by relationships.

Our ability to give and receive God's love—to relate in ways that reflect the self-giving, empowering, gracing nature of God—is formed in the matrix and mud of relationships. Our story shapes our faith. And to live in the story of God's love, we must be reshaped by communion with each other.

Suffering feels like getting lost in a forest while the rest of the church hikes ahead, and the vulnerability and dependency we encounter in ourselves when we lose the trail while dusk descends painfully exposes the goal for which we were created. We need others, chiefly God, to survive. We were made for interdependence, but most of us have forgotten how dependent we are.

One mercy of suffering might be its unearthing and refining of our deepest desires. It forces us to face what we most love. We become what we adore, and self-sufficiency reduces us to shadows of what we were made to be. In the limits of suffering, when autonomy crashes into the wall of our broken, needy bodies and splintering, shipwrecked faith, we discover what we most long for is a God who loves us no matter what. The complacency of ease can numb the sense of, and prevent the acknowledgment of, what we most crave: union with God. The solitude of suffering forces us to make peace with our loneliness, to sense our deepest longing is not simply relief but wholeness of life in God. In my lonely, lengthy, interior pain, I have come to long for and seek the invisible companionship of God.[31] The greatest desire of my heart is union with God.[32]

My sense and your sense of his companionship, however, cannot be sustained in solitude; it can only be sustained in community, in faces and friendship where we glimpse the larger, longer truth that God sees us. In the shadowy forest of suffering, when the way is unclear and the sound of solitude scares us to our very core, God is lighting a desire that will lead us home. Our longing to walk forward with friends is not weak, empty, or a dream that will only disappoint. It's the spark of our embodied, relational souls crying for their safe haven in God. In the dismay and pain of isolation, faith trusts its small cry for communion is the God-given longing that will guide us home.[33]

In both the silence of solitude and the faces of the faithful, God is forming his love in us. Henry Cloud describes the secure attachment of so thoroughly absorbing our mother's gaze of love as newborns that we can perceive ourselves as constantly loved in her absence; in the same way, God is forming in us a deeper, fuller knowledge that we are constantly, wholly loved.[34] Through our spiritual rebirth as daughters and sons of God, we are united to Christ and begin internalizing memories of God's love. Suffering does not block his love; it is the ground of dependence where we sense our need for it.

The irony of suffering is that experiencing weakness makes us more human, not less. We fear any loss of freedom will erase part of who we are. But it is in our need for others that we experience the heart of being human. When we encounter our limitations, losses,

....

31 Thomas Merton, *No Man Is an Island* (New York: Barnes and Noble, 1983), 228.
32 Henri J. M. Nouwen, *Here and Now: Living in the Spirit* (New York: Crossroad, 1994), 54–55.
33 Nouwen writes that the real danger is to distrust our desire for communion. In the absence of connection, we begin to shame ourselves for wanting it. But desire for love and connection is our God-given longing for home, for himself. Nouwen, *Here and Now*, 56.
34 Cloud, *Changes That Heal*, 70.

and basic needs for comfort and help, we encounter the truth that we were never intended to be independent. "Indeed, the body is not one part but many."[35]

I reject the notion that I am an individual being, built by the bulk of my successes, suffering in the wake of my failures, a tree rooted in determination or withering in its lack. We are not sole trees standing stalwart in an open field, rooted only as deep or wide as our effortful faith will grind into the ground. We are more aspen than oak, reaching skyward in hope, glorious in waving gold, both our beauty and survival formed and sustained in interdependence. A single aspen tree is connected to hundreds or thousands more by a network of roots so deep they can survive wildfires. Stemming from one seedling and held together by shared roots, aspen trees in a grove stand as a single organism. Our glory is derived from one source, our strength from shared roots.

Unlike the aspens in their quiet unity, we forget our shared source, roots, and wholeness. We live like single trees instead of a grove, and we blame each other's lack of sturdiness when storms tear down our branches. When the soil of one's life lacks what is needed to strengthen drooping arms so they can lift in faith, we judge instead of fertilize. We forget we are a single organism—one body—and alone we wither.

Christians who are suffering need the church's root system to sustain them, but far too few of us have experienced this. We need the nourishment of our shared roots. My wholeness is inextricably connected to yours. My hope is bound up in yours. My capacity to taste and see that the Lord is good is not a creation of my own determination but the fruit of willing, self-sacrificing love. I am one who hopes because I am one who has been shaped by the hopes of others, whose hurts are held in the hearts of others, and whose faith when fragile is augmented by the faith of those who are strong.

....
35 1 Cor. 12:14.

The point of faith was never for you to sustain yourself on your own. The point of faith is to form your entire, embodied, relational self, through weakness and dependence to realize you were made to know and be known. It is to shape you, through the presence of Christ and the physical presence of his people, to sit, stand, dance, and run together in the rhythm of the Trinity pulsating through all time, space, and matter to unite all things in love. You won't always remember this reverberating love and unparalleled story on your own, but even this is grace, as the thread of weakness pulls you farther into the loom where the Weaver's hands are forming the fabric of a cosmic wholeness that will last.

CHAPTER 4

EMOTION

Present to Pain, Receptive to Grace

Pain—is missed—in Praise

—EMILY DICKINSON, POEM 604

My eyes are worn out from crying.
LORD, I cry out to you all day long;
I spread out my hands to you.

—PSALM 88:9

I wake in pain. My feet hit the cool wooden floor, rigid from heel to toe. I walk slightly crumpled to the safe cushioning of the couch, where I can sink again.

The Word says joy comes in the morning, but I can't remember what it feels like to wake without weariness.

The world is waking in the cobalt blue of predawn, and I want to wake too, out of the stupor of a body that hurts, out of the soul fatigue of longing that, like embers, grounds me in the ashes of my own sadness. I want to want Jesus more than the elimination of pain and the alluring light of my phone, so I turn thin pages to the

Psalms, where I learn to want. My wanting is feeble, but in trading scrolling for approval on a screen for listening to the Person who bound himself to my pain, and me to his life, I feel a rising warmth. On the pages of my journal I let my deep-blue feelings merge with tangerine hope, forming desires into words that liberate and lift, the pen my confessor, the pages my sanctuary.

Morning is where I learn to want instead of long, and words form into hope like steam. I wake in pain. With words chosen, absorbed, and formed, I rise in hope.

Pain isn't the enemy, but it does feel like it. We tend to look at our discouragement as a problem to be solved instead of a place to be comforted. If pain precipitates a struggle to believe God is good, we think it must be a problem to push away. The main way most Christians know how to cope with difficulty is to paint pain with truth. When we see hopelessness in the eyes of our friends, we remind them God is faithful.

"He's working all of this together for your good."

"You just have to believe he has a purpose for your pain."

"You have to believe God is sovereign."

What if our reminders of truth are rough brushstrokes over a masterpiece-in-progress that must be witnessed to be made whole? What if our quick insistence of God's goodness is keeping us from experiencing his presence in the places we most fear he has abandoned us? What if our fear of facing suffering is keeping us from living?

While snow still coated the St. Louis ground in the winter of 2011, I finally found the first job I loved, a job that used the degree I had fought to receive, the credential that signaled to my soul I was a fighter who wouldn't let sickness keep her from achieving her dreams. After a short, depressing stint as an underpaid temp at a hospice organization, I found a position working for our church's community development nonprofit. Writing fundraising letters and stuffing envelopes and occasionally consulting about asset-based strategies felt like a stamp of approval. I mattered. I could contribute to the world. I had insight to offer and skills to use. The economy and my body couldn't hold me back.

Each day, I'd drive past Forest Park, where svelte runners in leggings and shorts started to seem less like objects of my envy and more like a possibility of my future. I'd glance at Washington University and picture myself in a classroom, deep in debate, head turned up in the glory of thoughts coming together, getting a master's in social work on the way to changing the world. Ryan and I joined a church small group, where, though we were the youngest by twenty years and the people were admittedly quirky, the burden of loneliness began to dissipate. I started to feel less afraid of paying the bills. On Saturdays we would wander the aisles of the Soulard Market hand in hand, splitting a croissant and gathering produce for the meals I'd create that week. On Sundays we had people to hug. We were no longer nameless faces with a flimsy future. We were making a life for ourselves, and I thought it was all straight from God's hand.

With each passing day of winter's long stretch to spring, wrapping my fingers around the black steering wheel became more difficult. The four-mile stretch between home and work started to feel like thirty. At work, I'd prop my chin up with my elbow and reposition and yawn my way through the day. The effort to keep my body erect embarrassed me; I wasn't sure how to be a twenty-two-year-old and let my new coworkers see that my body felt seventy. I'd fight back tears on my way home, afraid of losing everything we had barely started to enjoy, and then I'd hobble my way up to our cheap second-floor apartment and sink into the couch until Ryan got back from his day at seminary. The clash between his days and mine was like crimson mixed with green. He'd come up the stairs exhausted but buoyant with hope about our future, only to see me on the couch again, having barely held back my tears until the warmth of his embrace.

Ryan couldn't hold the full weight of my tears, and I couldn't bear the pain in my body dimming the light of each passing day. We both felt the energy of a good future disintegrating in the void between our two polarized bodies. The fear, pain, and anguish of my body shattering the shape of our future was sucking all the oxygen out of our newborn marriage. Ryan's empathy flickered like a candle near the end of its wick, and I added "pissed" to the top of the list of grievances I held against God but couldn't acknowledge out loud.

We quickly reached the emotional limits of our young marriage and found ourselves desperately emailing our pastors for advice. We set up a meeting with one of them in St. Louis and also started sharing about how bleak things had become with the pastor back in Chattanooga, Tennessee, who had married us. Walking into our pastor's office in St. Louis felt like failure but created relief. I revealed the tears I had kept hidden at my desk down the hall, and Ryan wrapped words around the helplessness he felt watching me hurt. I don't even remember that pastor's name, but I remember his acknowledgment of our vulnerability breathed enough courage into us to let our new community see our struggle. Simple dishes of home-cooked Chinese food showed up on our doorstep, and Trader Joe's frozen meals started to fill our freezer as our private sadness began to be shared by a small group of people we were just beginning to like, let alone trust.

It was uncomfortable and embarrassing but occasionally sweet, and the kindness infused us with just enough energy to move forward. With me unable to keep working, our seminary life in St. Louis was no longer affordable. God had called Ryan to become a pastor, and now it seemed he was allowing my body to turn Ryan's calling into a taunting mirage. My hands couldn't hold dishes at the sink, and our hearts couldn't hold a dream dissolving. Our pastor in Chattanooga asked us to consider moving back to serve alongside him at the church we had helped plant during our engagement. There was no paid position, but there was the safety of familiar faces and friendships with enough history to hold our faltering faith and help my fragile body with the basic necessities of life.

Ryan and I started our marriage with burning ambition, but suffering forced us to uncoil our hands from our good dreams. We left St. Louis one year into marriage with open hands, broken hearts, and a cornerstone of acceptance that looked like resignation and felt like failure. Autonomy dies hard.

Suffering slows the pace of our lives by exhuming our vulnerability. Bodies and souls experiencing lasting grief, disease, discouragement, and disappointment cannot help but struggle. Anxiety rumbles. Irritability rises. Groans abound. Suffering affects us, no matter how much ambition we possess.

Suffering was slowing our life, forcing us to be unmasked and destabilized. While our friends seemed to be on an upward trajectory, we were spending our days growing accustomed to tears, palpable sadness, and the frustrating reality of having one spouse too sick to do more than exist. It was an existential crisis as much as a crisis of our faith.

Slowing down our life to the pace of my disease was simply the beginning of a terrible, beautiful descent into the place where, I would find, God had already made his home.

⚓

The deepest anguish of suffering involves coming up against the divide in ourselves between believing God is loving and feeling it is true. It's the divide I encountered when sickness forced us to move back to Chattanooga for support, and the one you probably face again and again when life feels far from what you hoped it would be.

We learn early in life to dismiss our inner experience, thinking if we could believe the right things about God and pain and relationships, then our lives would be good. In our churches, homes, and friendships, we are much more comfortable approaching God through the domain of intellect than the realm of emotion, not realizing emotion guides the flow of our lives whether we acknowledge it or not.[1]

Reframing our thoughts about God will never be enough to cross the divide between our painful experiences and God's love.

Pain invites us into the canyon where we will be made whole. It brings us to the limits of our understanding of God and to the end of our sufficiency. Suffering walks us to the anxious edge of knowing God and asks us to instead be known by him. Our inability to think our way into hope is a grace, because hope comes through being known.

The divide in ourselves between our pain and our hope is illuminated by the divide in the hemispheres of our brains.[2] Here is where knowing and being known come together and where pain can begin to be transformed into praise. In Psalm 86:11, in the middle of distress, David asks a striking thing of God: "Teach me your way, LORD, and I will live by your truth. Give me an undivided mind to fear your name." To live by the truth, to find our way through the vast darkness of suffering, we need God to give us an undivided mind.

Our brains are made up of the left and right hemispheres, or sides. You've probably heard people refer to being more "right-brained" or "left-brained," but both sides represent ways of knowing

....

1   An overreliance on any one aspect of humanness in Christian practice and Christian community will lead to fragmented lives and broken hearts. A church that relies heavily on heightened emotion is just as disintegrated and dangerous as a church that is overly intellectual.

2   Curt Thompson, *Anatomy of the Soul: Surprising Connections between Neuroscience and Spiritual Practices That Can Transform Your Life and Relationships* (Carol Stream, IL: Tyndale, 2010), xvii, 33–37. This section draws from Thompson's summaries of the left and right sides of the brain.

and being that must be brought together in order for us to live with any amount of well-being.

The right side of the brain is more active than the left in the earliest months of life, building the neural connections babies need to begin forming a relationship with their mother (or primary caregiver), themselves, and the outside world. The right side of the brain forms the connections we need to be aware we have a body full of sensations existing in time and space among other bodies thrumming with nonverbal communication. It gives us the capacity to grasp an overall sense of experience, including the social and emotional tone of the context we occupy.

The left side of the brain becomes active slightly later than the right and forms our linear, logical, lingual, and literal processing. It helps us make sense of our experiences, including God's place in them, works hard to resolve any confusion we experience, gives us a sense of our individuality or separateness from others, and produces our ability to engage in right-versus-wrong thinking. The left side of the brain tends to dominate in situations in which we are searching for knowledge; not surprisingly, our questions of why suffering is happening and how we can make it stop certainly keep it firing.

Both sides of the brain are needed for us to be whole, but our culture fosters and rewards left-brained living, teaching us the path to security lies in knowing right from wrong. As we step into the gray fog of suffering, we come up against the limits of logical processing. Curt Thompson writes, "But when such analysis is the dominant mode by which we encounter other people or God . . . , joy becomes merely a defined concept. . . . However, the right mode of operation enables us to open ourselves to be touched by God and known *by* him in such a way as to become living expressions of love. The integration of the left and right systems is required to experience being known by someone else."[3]

....
3   Ibid., 37.

Expending vast amounts of mental energy on finding the reason you ache and grieve might be keeping you from being known and supported in your struggle. Grasping to find the purpose in your pain may be the very thing preventing you from experiencing comfort and even transformation in your suffering.

In Romans 12:2, Paul writes, "Do not be conformed to this age, but *be transformed by the renewing of your mind,* so that you may discern what is the good, pleasing, and perfect will of God" (emphasis added). Being transformed in life and in suffering must involve renewing our minds to know and be known with undivided brains. Whole brains, whole hearts, whole faith. We need the right side of our brains to lean toward trusting the God who says he is good.

Left-brained living says knowledge is what we need to be secure, but the gospel says being known by God is the security we long for.

In chapter 2 we discussed the importance of remembering the time we are at in the story of Scripture. Like remembering the time, remembering the truth matters, but there is more shaping our ability to remember and believe than we realize. The canyon between our pain and God's love feels wide because we each have a lifetime of experiences shaping our perceptions of God and our ability to navigate the rushing flood that seems to carry us into darkness.

Faithfulness in suffering requires radical honesty paired with remembrance of who God is. But how we "remember" God is far more complex than agreeing with the statement that God is good. Memory is forming the substance of your days and relationships every moment of every day, including how you experience God as either for you or against you, a concept we will explore in more depth in chapter 7.

You and I push away our pain by covering it with silence or an emphasis on truth that feels aspirational because we were created for communion but live in a story where independence appears to reign. The subtext of our suffering is shame—the dreadful sense that we are inadequate to deal with our lives. Individualism grasps for hope to respond to shame, producing social media slogans anxious to shine light into our shrouded souls: *You are enough. You are enough. You are enough.* The surprisingly good news is that we are not.

In the center of Scripture is a starkly different response to our suffering, a response that brings both sides of our brains together. The psalms show us being fiercely honest about not being enough is what creates and sustains intimacy with God. In chapter 2 we considered the way shame tells us a story that we will be alone, abandoned, and exposed, without any help but our own. The psalms offer a way to step into another story, where God pursues us with love, clothes us, and unites us to a power greater than our weakness. The Enemy is always leveraging shame to isolate us from God, ourselves, and one another. It masquerades as wisdom by stopping the flow of honesty in relationships through prioritizing the right words and thoughts about God over conversations seasoned with the salt and sweat of our humanness. The psalms invite us to be known by God in the substance of our inadequacy, and as they reveal our dependency again and again, trust becomes the structure of our souls.

We tend to hide our inability to cope with discouragement. The psalms provide an alternate pattern of basic, necessary, and transformative exposure. The witness of the psalms demonstrates remembering God in our pain by responding to him, the One who made us and seeks us. The psalms offer a conversational means of uniting mind and heart, honesty and truth, despair and hope, humans and their Maker.

We struggle to dwell in the tension between our pain and our need to praise, but the psalms hold us in a conversational traction.

Kathleen Norris writes, "This is the danger that lies hidden in Emily Dickinson's insight that 'Pain—is missed—in Praise': that we will try to jump too quickly from one to the other, omitting the necessary but treacherous journey in between, sentimentalizing both pain and praise in the process."[4] The psalms place us in paradox when we would rather detach from pain's pressure, and they show it is only in candor with our Maker that pain can dwell with praise.

Others might not be comfortable with our most honest, desperate cries, but the psalms make it exceedingly clear God is. This is the prayer book of God's people, written in the language of desire that situates our pain next to praise. Not hiding pain underneath praise. Not whispering about it. The psalms display God's people attuned to their pain and willing to express it in striking vulnerability, defeating "our tendency to try to be holy without being human first."[5] They show us how to speak what seems unwelcome inside the doors of a church, to speak to God with frustrated urgency, as David did in Psalm 83:1: "Do not be deaf, God; do not be quiet." This is not the language of presumption or arrogance; it is language of relationship, which lays the foundation of trust.

The language of the psalms is the primal language of need that forms trust, the relational matrix being created by the right hemisphere of the brain in a baby's earliest months of life. Describing the relational language of the psalms and how it teaches us to pray, Eugene Peterson writes, "It is the language we use naturally at and around the great nodal points of human life when our being is emergent or centered or questioned or endangered."[6] In our culture we are much more conversant in language that distances us from our vulnerability, forming the bulk of even our prayers around ideas and requests more than the underlying reality that our exist-

....
4   Kathleen Norris, *The Cloister Walk* (New York: Penguin, 1997), 94.
5   Ibid., 96.
6   Eugene H. Peterson, *Answering God: The Psalms as Tools for Prayer* (New York: HarperOne, 1991), 39.

ence depends on connection to another being.[7] We don't know how to communicate with God in the language of relationship, but the psalms offer us a way.

Here we find a response to God as the One who made us out of an overflow of his love, who is always seeking to enfold us in his care. The psalms show us how to acknowledge our pain with honesty. They teach us to approach God from the place of being undone instead of the prison of pretending we are self-sufficient and invulnerable. And in expressing our spitting frustration, derelict desperation, and arresting anguish, we mysteriously experience being heard. Relating to God as needy, moody, exhausted children forms hope, praise, and trust. Without vulnerability, the truth that God's love is steadfast remains abstract. Tears, groans, and sighs create the relational atmosphere where we can allow God to parent us. Weakness acknowledged and expressed forms trust.

Suffering shatters our illusions of immortality, and it is only in the shattering that we can come to know God and ourselves as we truly are.[8] Praying the psalms teaches us how to protest, be shattered, and praise in the midst of pain. Our protests over suffering betray belief in an illusion that we control our lives. Grace converts our protests over the absurdity and injustice of suffering into prayer. Protests become prayer, and prayer can turn into praise. As my friend Chuck DeGroat recently said, "The beauty of lamenting your pain is that your cynicism is refined into grief, your scapegoating is refined into trust, your anxiety is refined into rest."[9]

Right in the middle of the Word of God, we find that radical honesty about the true state of our souls creates beautiful remembrance that God relates to us with overflowing love. The psalms

....

7 Ibid., 36–40.
8 Henri J. M. Nouwen, *Reaching Out: The Three Movements of the Spiritual Life* (New York: Doubleday, 1986), 131.
9 Chuck shared this on Twitter recently and gave me his permission to quote it here. *https://twitter.com/chuckdegroat/status/997308089585078272.*

show God's children forming into their collective memory the reality that God hears them. Praying the psalms and allowing their honesty to animate our relationship with God causes this memory to be shaped in our lonely, frightened souls as well. In the fellowship of the psalms, inadequacy becomes the nativity of intimacy.

Learning about our divided minds, their need for wholeness, and the way Scripture gives us an example of being known in our vulnerability has brought us to a critical question: will we experience our pain or spend our lives avoiding it?

Cistercian monk Thomas Merton warns us, "Indeed, the truth that many people never understand, until it is too late, is that the more you try to avoid suffering, the more you suffer, because smaller and more insignificant things begin to torture you in proportion to your fear of being hurt. The one who does most to avoid suffering is, in the end, the one who suffers the most."[10]

God continuously invites us to know his presence in our pain, but we often miss his invitation because we are too busy dismissing his messengers.[11] When we paint over pain with insistence on truth, we are discarding the substance of our greatest comfort. Emotion is the landscape of experiencing God's presence, but most of us don't know how to tread its ground. When we quickly exhort ourselves or others to believe truth, we walk past the trails that lead to our healing.

The only way the descent of suffering becomes beautiful is through learning to listen to and respond to our emotions. Think of emotion as energy in motion. Emotion is the energy that guides

---

10 Thomas Merton, *The Seven Storey Mountain* (Boston: Houghton Mifflin Harcourt, 1999), 91.
11 Thompson, *Anatomy of the Soul*, 95.

and organizes your brain.[12] Whether you consider yourself an emotional person or not, emotion fuels your life. Rather than a thing to be bewildered by or ashamed of, emotion is the spark God created to most move you toward himself. Your difficult emotions are not a barrier to joy; they are a conduit to receiving the love of God in your innermost being.

Long before we have the words sadness, fear, or shame to describe the way we feel, our bodies are responding to the world of stimuli around us. Our brains assess the shifts in our environment to determine how to respond according to the level of perceived safety or attraction. Emotion is first and foremost preparing us for action through the way our brains constantly assess and appraise the world around us. Our bodies respond to these rapid-fire appraisals, forming sensations and perceptions that give us awareness of a shift happening within ourselves, shifts that generally are originating from the lower regions of our brains that are not immediately connected to our conscious awareness. We first experience emotion through sensory perceptions and physical behaviors, like the flush of our face, the shaking in our hands, or a heaviness in our chest. We may automatically respond with a sigh, with a groan, by looking down, or by tightening our shoulders. What is perceived by the lower regions of the brain is swiftly reinforced in the body, carrying the flow of emotion through us and into our relationships. As we become conscious of these shifts, and when they persist, we experience an awareness of our feelings—anger, fear, shame, sadness, guilt, joy.

The emotional energy inside each of us can seem obtrusive, threatening, or confusing, and this is largely because we learned to experience and evaluate emotion in our families of origin. Their emotional volatility or even lack of emotional expression impacts

....
12 Ibid., 90. The following section draws from the work of Thompson in describing the nature of emotion, particularly chapter 6 of *Anatomy of the Soul* (pp. 89–108).

the way we experience how safe and good emotions are. But judging or distancing ourselves from emotions will only limit our ability to experience God's presence in our pain. Emotion guides our lives whether we give it our attention or not. Judging emotion as bad or dismissing its presence in your life only increases its power to control you.

Emotions are reflections of something central to the heart of God, the One who allows himself to be impacted by us. God feels grief,[13] joy,[14] compassion,[15] pity,[16] love,[17] and hate.[18] God is far more comfortable with emotion than we are. To find our way to joy and hope in suffering, we must follow his example instead of the minimizing, dismissive norms of our culture.[19]

Shame will always try to minimize or magnify our emotions in suffering, but God invites us to pay appropriate attention to them as a lens through which we can see him. First Corinthians 6:19 tells us our bodies are temples of the Holy Spirit. Our bodies are the place where God has chosen to dwell. As we become more aware of the thousands of shifts happening in our bodies every day, we become more capable of treating our bodies as the place of worship God calls them. When witnessed with awareness, our painful and pleasant emotions and sensations can become the place we realize God resides in us. Practicing mindful awareness of our emotions can change our brain structure, rewiring neural pathways that used to lead us into despair into pathways of peace.[20] Turning toward our

....

13 Gen. 6:6; Ps. 78:40.

14 Isa. 62:5; Zeph. 3:17; Jer. 32:41.

15 Deut. 32:36; Ps. 135:14.

16 Judg. 2:18.

17 Jer. 31:3; John 3:16.

18 Pss. 5:5; 11:5; Prov. 6:16. This is just a sampling of God's emotions in Scripture, rather than an exhaustive list. To consider the emotions of God further, see Stephen Voorwinde, *Jesus' Emotions in the Gospels* (London: T&T Clark, 2011).

19 Thompson, *Anatomy of the Soul*, 90.

20 Lisa L. Baldini et al., "The Clinician as Neuroarchitect: The Importance of Mindfulness and Presence in Clinical Practice," *Clinical Social Work Journal* 42, no. 3 (2014): 221.

painful emotions with nonjudgmental awareness can be the very act that over time transforms us by renewing our minds.

We can turn toward the pain of suffering because God has turned toward us. "Our brokenness is often so frightening to face," Henri Nouwen reminds us, "because we live it under the curse. Living our brokenness under the curse means that we experience our pain as a confirmation of our negative feelings about ourselves."[21] We don't have to live in a cycle of negative reinforcement, fearing our suffering, avoiding its presence, and then feeling detached from God's love if suffering doesn't cease. "We have the mind of Christ."[22] Because God has turned toward us in Christ, we can turn toward our pain. And when we do, our minds are renewed to be like his.

Maybe turning toward pain is a form of repentance, *metanoia*. Maybe suffering, with its steady flood of pain and sorrow to turn toward, makes you and me more ready to be whole.

Leaning toward pain is not a lesson that, once learned, gets left behind like the third grade and its schoolbooks. My small story, like yours, is nested in a larger narrative, a narrative in process, where the powers of darkness still sway and startle my mind and heart even though the end of the story has been written.[23] I know pain and sadness and weakness are an invitation to be held, but my body still lives in the shadows where pain is an enemy to kill or deny or ignore. A decade into days full of pain, and I still push back against its presence. I still resist the place where I know God will meet me.

....
21 Henri J. M. Nouwen, *Life of the Beloved* (New York: Crossroad, 1992), 96.
22 1 Cor. 2:16.
23 I first came across the phrase "nested narrative" in a journal article: Jason Walch, "Nested Narratives: Interpersonal Neurobiology and Christian Formation," *Christian Education Journal* 12, no. 1 (2015): 151-61.

Pain, shame, and sadness remain places of tension in the landscape of my life, gravel-strewn quarries whose jagged cliffs and depths appear fearsome, where mining feels like cruel self-robbery, and also where the light of love catches the edges of what looked blunt, scattering belovedness as through a prism. When I kneel toward the small, scattered stones of sorrow or shame or grief, ordinary time lived in the boundaries of sixty-second minutes is penetrated by the Love that transcends time.

But sixty-second minutes have long synchronized my soul to the rhythm of scarcity, and when reminders of weakness swiftly come, I'm apt to avoid the quarry. I skirt its edges. I turn my back to the glinting, sharp objects below, looking instead at the mountain of accomplishment I'd rather conquer. The tasks I'd like to finish. The dishes that need to be done. The emails to return. The people to speak with. But the mountain of all I wish I could do or achieve is only another face of fear disconnecting me from me. All the tasks are hills in the ascension of my kingdom, and my kingdom is a crumbling, insatiable lie. The flush of my face, the knot in my chest, and the embarrassment of falling tears are each an echo calling me home to acknowledge, remember, and hope instead for a kingdom that lasts.

I am a perpetual third grader with a master's degree in avoidance, in a body held in tension between her coming redemption and a pile of rocky emotions and sensations that frighten, compel, isolate, and integrate. I know leaning toward pain will turn these stones into instruments that play redemption's song, but I turn away from what I know to maintain my illusory dominion over my small kingdom of ease. Why do I resist pain when I know grace is near?

The ancient, unfolding story tells me God is patient and grace is relentless, and though my heart plucks out a tune of self-sufficiency, the stones of pain are teaching me to sing a stronger song. This is not a lesson to master but a tension in which to thrive.

I most resist the grace of God not through believing he isn't good but in ignoring or avoiding the messengers of my soul through which he seeks my attention. My inner sensations, perceptions, and emotions are the cacophony of sound the world tells me to dismiss but God invites me to hear.

Jesus says, "Come to me, all of you who are weary and burdened, and I will give you rest."[24] Jesus acknowledges your burden. He doesn't shame it, doesn't label it, and doesn't proclaim it a barrier to being a faithful Christian. With outstretched hand, he invites you to rest. But first you must acknowledge what he already sees with his open, kind eyes. To receive the rest Jesus offers, you must first acknowledge your weariness and your burden.

Shame powerfully works to block us from acknowledging our weariness by questioning its validity, labeling it as too much, spiritualizing it as bad, pointing out how everyone else seems to be fine, and turning our eyes toward all the shiny things we should be expending energy on to produce and control and sustain. It's almost like shame wants us to be God . . .

Dismissal of pain will only block you from the love you were made for. Your wounds need tending, not ignoring. As Henri Nouwen encourages, "It is important that you dare to stay with your pain and allow it to be there."[25] The place of your weariness is the place Jesus stretches out his hand to enter the good reality of a story where he is God and you are not. God is not inviting you to cognitively understand why you have experienced loss. He is inviting you to feel and know his care for you as your Father. Choose to try believing that pain is something God wants you to pay attention to.[26]

....

24 Matt. 11:28.
25 Henri J. M. Nouwen, *The Inner Voice of Love: A Journey through Anguish to Freedom* (New York: Image, 1999), 47.
26 This sentence originally appeared in K.J. Ramsey, "The Painful Part of Wholeness," *Catalyst Leader* (October 17, 2018), *https://catalystleader.com/read/the-painful-part-of-wholeness*.

Just as the example of the psalmists demonstrates, God invites us to acknowledge the true state of our souls. Turning toward our pain and crying out to ask God to turn toward it as well creates a space of grace where the echoes of redemptive history become personal and present sounds of comfort. In dependence, we learn how to trust. In trust, we learn to keep trusting. God's kindness toward his people throughout all history becomes structured in our emotional memory when we relate to him from our places of pain.

Gently turning toward the thing you most fear, knowing God has already turned toward it with love and acceptance, will be the continuous reversal that defrauds suffering of its power to disrupt, diminish, and defeat you.

CHAPTER 5

THE CLOUD

Suffering Is Transformational Space

God is not absent. He is everywhere in the world we
are too dispirited to love. . . . All too often the task
to which we are called is . . . letting grace wake love
from our intense, self-enclosed sleep.

—CHRISTIAN WIMAN, *MY BRIGHT ABYSS*

May my mind come alive today
To the invisible geography
That invites me to new frontiers,
To break the dead shell of yesterdays,
To risk being disturbed and changed.

—JOHN O'DONAHUE, *TO BLESS THE SPACE BETWEEN US*

One weekend this February we drove to Chattanooga, Tennessee, to visit some of our dearest friends. Their house sits at the base of Lookout Mountain, where on a clear day you can see the outline of limestone cliffs and homes high above. Farther down their road you can see Covenant College, where we all met, with Carter Hall's spire and the chapel's largeness stark against the sky, like pinnacles of hope.

Most of the weekend, the mountain was a rising mass of brown and green trees veiled in a gray, dense cloud with no top in sight. One day Ryan and I drove to our alma mater to visit with a former professor, winding our way into the cloud, into the place where mist obscures a gorgeous view, sometimes so impenetrably you can't see farther than five to ten feet.

Every winter Lookout Mountain lives in a cloud. At first it's almost dreamlike. But the initial magic of mist quickly fades into the sadness of a sunless sky, an obscurity that feels like it could stretch on forever. Our friend worked in student life for more than a decade at the college and shared that each winter, rates of depression and anxiety soar among students.

It's hard to exist in a cloud for very long.

Suffering brings us again and again to opaque places of confusion and frustration. We experience both long seasons of darkness and sudden storms of lightning-like fear. We repeatedly find ourselves in the foggy incomprehensibility of circumstances that make it difficult to sense God's presence. Our eyes see a mountain with no peak, an ascent with no trail, a fierce landscape no one wants to occupy.

But it is in the cloud that we are transformed.

In the last chapter, we considered how leaning toward our pain can be the place where we find our greatest comfort. We discussed God's startlingly beautiful affirmation of our emotions as a good, necessary part of our humanness reflecting his own heart. Perhaps you have become slightly more persuaded that emotions are a good and even beautiful part of who you are and how you can know and be known by God. But knowing emotions are good and experiencing them as such when suffering takes us again and again to the place of our weary weakness are two different things. It is difficult to keep turning toward the place we fear when we have to go there so frequently.

Our present discomfort has to be united with God's past faithfulness to create future hope, but we struggle to allow our current distress to be touched by God's faithfulness shown to us in Christ. We all have sustained critical wounds that keep us stuck, expecting God to be absent, indifferent, or tyrannical and expecting ourselves to be stronger and more sufficient than we are. We defend ourselves against turning toward the place of our pain, because it triggers our primal fears of being disconnected from love, security, and belonging. We can't gently turn toward the place where God will meet and heal us if we don't let ourselves acknowledge we are there in the first place. In this chapter, we'll explore how to notice and inhabit the clouded, confusing place of suffering. Toward the end, we'll walk through a short exercise connecting what you learned in the previous chapter with a practical way to acknowledge and name your emotions.

During the same trip to Chattanooga, I visited one of my college roommates whom I hadn't seen in years and listened as she shared the surprising way time has shaped her. Wrapping her hands around a cup of Earl Grey, Elizabeth looked up with a mixture of wonder and amusement and reminisced, "When we were in college, I remember learning how suffering was part of the Christian life, but I had never experienced it."

She carefully lifted her steaming tea and laughed. "I remember thinking I wasn't ready for Jesus to come back because I wanted to get married and have kids. There was so much good I wanted to experience in life first!"

She nearly rolled her eyes, and a kind, self-deprecating smile swept across her face as she confessed, "I remember thinking, 'Oh my, I hope suffering can wait for a while at the very least!'"

Tears formed in Elizabeth's eyes as she looked into mine and shared how starkly the last several years had diverged from her expectations. Every six to twelve months for nearly a decade, she had faced another massive loss, trauma, or painful change that would remain part of her life forever. From years of aching for children, to feeling family relationships shift and splinter in the wake of shared trauma, to watching her brother lose his fight to aggressive cancer, Elizabeth had come to know intimately suffering was not a distant possibility or short-term delay she could conquer or simply move past on the way to all she wanted.

Instead, she shared, suffering had somehow brought some of the most beautiful relationships in her life. Wondering aloud, Elizabeth admitted she still found herself treating suffering like an obstacle or source of shame cutting her off from good. Setting down her tea, she conceded, "It's hard to stay in the place suffering takes me."

Suffering is like a terrifying mountain whose peak is covered in clouds. We find ourselves midway in an ascent we did not choose. The path is strewn with rocks and bordered by sudden cliffs. The way forward is uncertain, unsafe. Our lungs burn to breathe in the thin air. How did we get here? Is a rescue coming?

Suffering breaks our hearts wide open, and the overflow of sorrow, anger, and anxiety terrifies us. Both our raw tears and our apathetic silence startle us in their pure intensity. How far such feelings seem from hearts that trust their Father! Hopelessness terrifies us, we who are supposed to be marked by hope. The senselessness of suffering gnaws at our souls, making us feel helpless and stuck. All our prayers, all our tears, and all the books we read to make sense of the senseless cannot lift the cloud hovering over the purpose of our pain.

Even as we ache, our bodies remember their original intention—union with their Maker. They are vessels made to collect, retain, and run over with God's love. We were not created to suffer; as my husband has said, we are haunted by our original goodness. We want to escape the terrible cloud of suffering because it feels antithetical to being human. We want to escape suffering because we were not made for pain. We were made for love.

We wish suffering were a fixed point in time we could get past, but it is actually a place we find ourselves. It is a country we visit without wanting to, sometimes for long seasons. It is the cloudland we step into when anxiety screams all is not well, illness threatens mutiny once again, and relationships remain tainted by lack.

Suffering is a place we will repeatedly find ourselves in as we journey toward the wholeness God has for us in his kingdom. Whether we try to escape it or pretend we aren't there, suffering is a place we will repeatedly occupy as we await the return of Jesus and the restoration he will bring.

Suffering is not a detour or a delay but the place where Love finds us.

Suffering is a place where what feels like absence is actually a safe haven where the truest love is formed.

Rather than the place we lose our selves, suffering is the place we find them.[1]

Suffering brings us to the threshold of who we are becoming. It walks us to the edges of our hearts, confronting us with the

....
1   My friend Adam Young has a brilliant podcast with a title similar to this phrase, *The Place We Find Ourselves*. Adam's podcast explores themes similar to the ones in this book, around the integration of narrative, theology, psychology, and interpersonal neurobiology in the healing of trauma. Adam Young, *The Place We Find Ourselves*, https://adamyoungcounseling.com/podcast/.

vulnerability we would normally want to ignore. It shoves us to the margins of our relationships, where our sadness or lack of improvement frustrates those we know. It elbows us into the borderlands of our relationship with God, where things we used to find comfort or joy in now feel empty. It presses us to the periphery of our personalities, where we're fine one moment and full of fear the next. Suffering brings us to liminal, transitional space.[2]

The French anthropologist Arnold van Gennep coined the term "liminality" to describe a stage in rites of passage, such as the transition from childhood to adulthood, when we are not one thing but we also are not the other.[3] In liminal space we are "betwixt and between the positions assigned and arrayed by law, custom, convention."[4] I am someone with a disease, and I am more than my disease. I am capable, and I am limited. I have deep hope, and sometimes I'm hopeless. I exist in the space between the poles of my experience, and suffering creates startling polarity. In suffering that lingers, we experience an ongoing, shifting sense of who we are, sometimes reconciling ourselves with our pain and sometimes distancing ourselves from it. Rather than a one-time biographical disruption, long-term suffering can be a continuous, unfolding disruption.[5]

Suffering repeatedly brings us to liminal spaces where we stand at the threshold of who we were and who we are becoming, and the experience can be mystifying and terrifying. We are no longer the people we were before suffering started, and we long for the freedom we thought we had before things became so hard. You might wonder if you just need to grit your teeth until God finally returns to make everything right.

Priest and author Richard Rohr describes the distress we feel

....
2   *Limen* in Latin means "threshold."
3   Arnold van Gennep, *The Rites of Passage* (New York: Routledge, 2013), 10.
4   Victor Turner, *The Ritual Process: Structure and Anti-Structure* (Piscataway, NJ: Transaction, 2011), 95.
5   Marja-Liisa Honkasalo, "Vicissitudes of Pain and Suffering: Chronic Pain and Liminality," *Medical Anthropology* 19, no. 4 (2001): 319.

in the liminality of suffering: "Liminality occurs when you have left the tried and true, but have not yet been able to replace it with anything else. It is when you are between your old comfort zone and any possible new answer. If you are not trained in how to hold anxiety, how to live with ambiguity, how to entrust and wait, you will run . . . anything to flee this terrible 'cloud of unknowing.'"[6]

When we experience suffering that does not cease, we sometimes feel locked in a soundproof room. We kick and pound against the walls to escape, but all our efforts to stop the experience of suffering leave us with bruises and disappointment instead of rescue and relief. Our cries ricochet off the walls, making us question whether God or anyone hears us. Feeling abandoned in cloudy circumstances that seem to stretch on forever is almost too hard to bear. In resentment, defeat, or exhaustion, we stop crying and start numbing. Cue Netflix. Pour another glass of wine. We numb, pretend, and ignore the pain and place of suffering because we feel incapable of facing our clouded lives. Deeper still, we fear being cut off from God's love.

Suffering places us in obscurity, where we cannot see God's purposes or presence clearly. When all the hard things stay in our lives instead of fading into the past, we may repeatedly experience what Christians through the ages have described as a dark night of the soul.[7] Here God can seem distant, joy a lost jewel, and faith a pile of disassembled parts. We wonder if God has abandoned us. Or is he punishing us?

We were made for union with God and beautiful connection to one another, but suffering can make us feel utterly disconnected.

6   Richard Rohr, "Grieving as Sacred Space," *Sojourners* 31, no. 1 (January 2002): 22.
7   Gerald May, *The Dark Night of the Soul: A Psychiatrist Explores the Connection between Darkness and Spiritual Growth* (New York: HarperOne, 2004), 26.

Because every relationship in our world has been fractured by sin, we all find ways to manage the vulnerability of disconnection. We were made for relationships, but because of the fall, our relationships are never adequate to fill the gaping hole in our hearts, the desire for belonging and security. Underneath our fear in suffering is our deepest desire to be known and loved by God. We so fear being met with an eternal darkness that we anesthetize our anxiety with beliefs, behaviors, and attitudes that give a temporary hit of relief but never satiate our deepest need.

When the fog of suffering hovers over our lives, we are often subconsciously shoved back in time to places of earlier wounding. Our early experiences, including ones we don't have words for or have downplayed as insignificant, steer our way forward through the fog. We respond to the confusing pain of suffering in the ways we responded in childhood to being neglected, intruded upon, overlooked, or abandoned.

Evil distracts us from turning toward the place we fear by whispering the original lie of self-sufficiency. We assume our private pain is faithlessness to hide or a burden to shoulder alone. If we cannot keep ourselves from suffering, if we cannot summit the mountain of pain, we will at least privatize our suffering until it can be conquered.

We come to the place of suffering sweating under the weight of the jam-packed baggage of strategies we've used to cope with insecurity our entire lives. The tools we use to escape or dispel the fog of suffering are the same we've always used to try to protect ourselves from pain in life. Whether you view yourself as strong and secure or frightened and weak, you have found comfort in patterns of relating, in possessions, and in belief systems that temporarily shield you from the harshness of feeling disconnected from God and others.

Suffering unpacks our baggage, exposing the strategies we've always used to keep ourselves from feeling vulnerable. We spend so much of life busying ourselves to avoid feeling empty, amassing wealth to avoid feeling out of control, reading books to avoid seeming incompetent, and growing a career to avoid feeling purposeless. We find security in power, knowing the right answers, appearing interesting, and filling our time and bellies with exciting experiences and flavors. We fill ourselves with all that is not God to stomach the emptiness of not having what our souls were made for—perfect, complete, faithful love.

We face the terrible mountain of suffering and try to either ascend or descend on our own. Holding the ambiguity of long-term suffering feels like death; so we try to create our own comfort, our own rescue.

We reach out with weary arms to peel back the curtains of darkness looming in our lives. But in our reaching, darkness thickens. Our methods of escape are the machine of our discouragement, because they inevitably turn us back to ourselves instead of toward the relationships where our hopes can be held. As Kelly Kapic writes, sin "actually bends or curves us upon ourselves (*homo incurvates in se*). We were designed to embrace God and others, but instead we are now consumed with ourselves."[8] To evade the cloud, we end up building fortress walls around ourselves, further distancing us from the love we long for. The ways we try to escape suffering exacerbate the suffering itself.

I tried to escape the cloud of my suffering through the twisted pride of uniqueness. When I didn't see anyone else whose life looked like mine, I believed my suffering was something no one could understand. I thought I was the only one I knew who was

8   Kelly M. Kapic, *God So Loved, He Gave* (Grand Rapids: Zondervan, 2010), 37. Here Kapic references Martin Luther's insights on original sin.

so afflicted. I couldn't bear the cloud obscuring the meaning of my pain, so in the absence of meaning, I created some. *God must have a special purpose for my pain.* While my friends were trifling away at things that surely didn't matter as much, I believed I was special, awakened to the reality of pain in the world.[9] By believing my suffering was somehow special, I set myself up to differentiate myself from others instead of attaching to them. By so wanting a purpose in my pain, I placed distance between myself and Christ's body. In losing my old life, I needed purpose and identity, but I tried to find it by elevating my uniqueness. Here is sin: acquiring my identity in contrast and opposition to other human beings.[10]

Another way of trying to escape is believing a lie that goes like this: "I don't get to share my suffering with others because I'm responsible to care for others. I just have to suck it up because other people need me." Sometimes we avoid feeling the real pain and discomfort in our lives by trying to refocus our energy on others. Minimizing our suffering as though it were not important, or because we just don't have time to feel sad, or because we should be strong for our families and friends is just another form of pride. When we distance ourselves from our pain, we end up distancing ourselves from everyone. Suffering set aside again and again to help others becomes a burning ball of resentment toward the people we love and the God who made us.

Most of us see the cloud over the purpose of our pain and try to blow back the fog by finding an explanation. We devour knowledge about our suffering because we fear we might be devoured by our suffering. The gray tinge of suffering leads us to color in our confusing circumstances with crayons of our own making. *I think God is teaching me . . .*

....

9 As my North-Carolina-born-and-raised mother-in-law would say, bless my [ridiculous] heart.

10 John Zizioulas, *Communion and Otherness: Further Studies in Personhood and the Church* (New York: T&T Clark, 2006), 229–30.

We think that if we could find the reason we're stuck in suffering, maybe we could learn the lesson and leave. The lack of answers and largeness of loss pierce our bodies with the fury of chaos. The incessant urge to spiritualize pain undervalues our embodied experience of it. Searching hard for what God might be teaching us is more indicative of anxiety than faith. When we grasp for tidy lessons or search tirelessly for some hidden sin we might never find, we are doing penance for a pain God already carried. Searching for the hidden lesson in our suffering detaches us momentarily from feeling the pain, but feeling our pain is where we can be known, grown, and filled with the hope we need.

When we overspiritualize our suffering, we turn our hearts away from the sacred mystery of how God is forming us in our suffering. Reflecting on having cancer, psychiatrist Gerald May writes, "I don't have to look for spiritual lessons in every trouble that comes along. There have been many spiritual lessons to be sure, but they've been given to me in the course of life; I haven't had to figure out a single one."[11]

In the absence of a lesson, we try to create our own purpose. No one wants to admit it, but sometimes we channel our frustration about senseless suffering into plans to dazzle the world with our overcoming. We'll make something of our suffering; we'll profit from the pain. We'll find our own remedies and sell their half-acting good to others. We'll buy the essential-oil starter kit, secretly hoping we'll be the next success story on Instagram. Or we'll be beach body coaches, exercising our way out of sadness, pumping past our lingering questions about why God would allow our stories to hurt. Trying to turn clouds into sparkling rain only further divides our hearts from hope that lasts. The cloud of suffering is too thick for our effort. All the effort will leave you empty, with the cloud still looming. What will you chase then?

....
11 May, *Dark Night of the Soul*, 2–3.

Our unique ways of escaping and avoiding suffering are rooted in a self-sufficiency that will never be enough. And, hallelujah, this is good news.

Suffering is not a mark on the timeline of your life. It is not a season with a clear beginning and end, or a problem you can overcome. It is a place you will visit again and again, a place whose clouds threaten and frighten but whose landscape can bring you nearer to your true home.

"Sometimes the only way we can enter the deeper dimensions of the journey is by being unable to see where we are going," Gerald May writes.[12] In the cloud, our layers of striving are dissolved. Our carefully crafted self-image of success and independence is being worn away. All that is not our true self—the self hidden with Christ in God—is being removed, often in ways we cannot entirely see or comprehend. On the confounding ground of our suffering, we are being transformed in what sometimes feels like complete darkness. As May writes, "God darkens our awareness *in order to keep us safe*."[13] Under cloud cover, we find the limits of our old ways of knowing God. Identities built on striving crumble into dust. In the mist, God gently removes the tattered clothing we've sewn to cover our shame and re-dresses us in royal robes.

In the place of suffering, we are stripped of our attachments to all that is not God so we can attach to God instead.[14] Communion with God is formed and strengthened in the cloud, not just in the sun. The cloudland we come to is both fierce and gentle, frightening and holy, confusing and creative. Therapist and author Dan Allender writes of this place as a desert we must pass through to find wholeness: "It is

12 Ibid., 72.
13 Ibid.
14 Ibid., 51.

in the silence of the desert that we hear our dependence on noise. It is in the poverty of the desert that we see clearly our attachments to the trinkets and baubles we cling to for security and pleasure. The desert shatters the soul's arrogance and leaves body and soul crying out in thirst and hunger. In the desert we trust God or die."[15]

In suffering, God recapitulates and refines the stories of our lives, where our raiments of striving were first woven, bringing us to spaces of infant-like dependency that burn away our adult illusions of sufficiency.[16] This is where we partner with God to "take off your former way of life, the old self that is corrupted by deceitful desires, to be renewed in the spirit of your minds, and to put on the new self, the one created according to God's likeness in righteousness and purity of the truth."[17]

The place where we feel abandoned is the place where we are transformed. Here "in the darkness, way beneath our senses, God is instilling 'another, better love' and 'deeper, more urgent longings' that empower our willingness for all the necessary relinquishments along the way."[18]

The cloud of suffering is not a storm. It's a shelter. It's a studio. It's the mysterious place where we are made new.

God is here. He has not left. He is like the father in the parable of the prodigal son, patiently waiting for his son to return. God is not

15 Dan Allender, *The Healing Path: How the Hurts in Your Past Can Lead You to a More Abundant Life* (Colorado Springs: Waterbrook, 2000), 21.

16 David Brooks agrees, writing, "Finally, suffering shatters the illusion of self-sufficiency, which is an illusion that has to be shattered if any interdependent life is going to begin. Seasons of pain expose the falseness and vanity of most of our ambitions and illuminate the larger reality of living and dying, caring and being cared for. Pain helps us see the true size of our egotistical desires." David Brooks, *The Second Mountain: The Quest for a Moral Life* (New York: Random House, 2019), 37.

17 Eph. 4:22–24.

18 May, *Dark Night of the Soul*, 73.

on the other side of our suffering. He is in it. The invisible God is closer to us than we are to ourselves.[19]

We can't inhabit and experience the place where God shelters and transforms us if we do not know where we are. Faith begins in recognizing the cloud and noticing we've lost our way. It is a response to the God who is more present than we feel, asking us to name the place we find ourselves in. Every day, God asks us to answer the question he asked Adam and Eve in Genesis 3: *Where are you?*

We locate the place we find ourselves in by noticing our emotions, our bodies, and our inner dialogue. Faith is a response that requires paying attention to ourselves.

A common bit of advice we get in suffering is to think more about others, to get our minds off ourselves. We are transformed not by thinking less about ourselves but by thinking differently about ourselves. Transformation happens in paying attention to our lives with kindness and compassion rooted in the care of a God who so loved us that he died for us. We are often taught holiness involves thinking less about ourselves and more about Jesus. We need Jesus—oh, how we need Jesus!—but we need him in the substance of our lives, in the emotional floods and deserts, in the places where we feel most abandoned, overwhelmed, and lifeless. Believing you need to think less about yourself may be leading you farther away from experiencing the presence of God refashioning you into the likeness of Christ. By judging our lives instead of inhabiting them, we miss dwelling in the place where God silently clothes us in his redeeming love.

To dwell there, we first need to gain awareness that something is off. This may seem so obvious it hurts, but I think most of us spend a great deal of our mental energy suppressing awareness of how we feel. *Where are you?* Life will continue to bring up situations that evoke distress. Noticing our distress rather than dismissing or

....
19 Thomas Merton, *No Man Is an Island* (New York: Barnes and Noble, 1983), 238.

ignoring it is the first way we can respond to God's invitation into the canyon of wholeness.

Emotional awareness is an underdeveloped muscle for many of us, one that can feel uncomfortable to use. As you learn to use it, as you begin using the functions of your left brain to notice the world of your right brain, you will experience gains that make the cloud of suffering more navigable, calm more accessible, and comfort more palpable.

One way I walk many of my clients through learning to be more aware of their feelings is by having them pay attention to their thoughts and how they connect to their physical sensations, as in the following exercise. We do not always have time to walk through a full exercise like this, but we can become more attuned to the distressing thoughts, sensations, and feelings we experience. When we take time to acknowledge how our bodies feel, we learn the feelings we so fear are not quite as scary as we thought. When we notice them, name them, and breathe deep in their presence, we invite the peace of God into the place of our pain.

- What are some thoughts you keep coming back to about this (this situation, experience, memory, etc.)? Narrow it down to one recurring thought. *I'm never going to feel better.*
- Now sit up straight with both of your feet planted firmly on the ground. Take a few deep breaths. In and out. Fully expand your belly and then let all of the air out. Take a few more of these deep breaths.
- Recall the thought you just noticed a minute ago. *I'm never going to feel better.* Notice how your body feels as you dwell on that thought. What sensations are you experiencing? (Take a minute to slowly scan your entire body, from the top of your head to the soles of your feet.) *A knot in my chest. Tightness in my shoulders. My body feels heavy.*
- Sometimes our physical sensations can guide us to recognizing and naming our feelings. What feelings might you be

experiencing in light of these sensations? (You might want to utilize a feelings wheel or emotions list, which are readily available online, to name what you are feeling.[20]) *Anxiety. Hopelessness. Abandonment.*

• Now that you have named some of your feelings, take a moment to acknowledge them. You don't have to run away from painful feelings. As you take several more deep, full breaths, acknowledge the feelings you just named. One by one. (You can even say, "Hello, anxiety," breathe deep for a few breaths to sit in its presence, then say, "Hello, hopelessness," breathe deep for a few breaths, and so on.)

Practicing mindful awareness of our emotions through exercises like this one or through cultivating a regular meditation or contemplative prayer practice can grow our capacity to answer God's question, *Where are you?* As we identify the place we find ourselves in, we can remember he is with us. When we give our distressing emotions kind attention instead of dismissing them or shaming ourselves for having them, we extend ourselves the loving presence of the God who comes to find us, just as he came pursuing Adam and Eve.

Suffering is a place we occupy. If we are not aware of the place we find ourselves in, we will be occupied by it instead. Counterintuitively, when we practice turning toward the place we fear, by naming our emotions and breathing deep in their presence, our minds calm down. We start to feel more like ourselves.

Walking into cloud cover, onto the rough ground of our pain, brings us into the experience of grace re-creating us. Within the

....

20 You can't know what you don't name. Here is an excellent feelings wheel to use along with this exercise: *https://www.thejuntoinstitute.com/blog/the-junto-emotion-wheel-why-and-how-we-use-it.*

clouds, through our tears, we look for the shape of grace nourishing this dying world with new life.

When the cares of my heart are many, ignoring their weight will only make them heavier. Finding my way to blue skies will only happen through first being honest about the clouded space I occupy. I have to acknowledge the lump in my chest telling me I might never finish writing this book. I need to notice the tiredness in my body, how I wake feeling like I haven't slept at all. I must be honest about how little the Word sparked encouragement in my heart this week. I have to notice and name the things I most dislike in order to find grace right here. When my strength evaporates like dew in the desert, I need renewal.

Today I felt darkness sticking to my soul. Self-doubt coiled around me like a boa constrictor, choking off my hope. I knew I needed to give my darkness space to breathe in the light alongside beauty. So after I noticed and named how I was doing, Ryan and I drove in search of light, to a botanical garden fifteen minutes away.

As we stepped into the misty greenhouse world of cultivated beauty, I let out my first deep exhalation of the day. My sad, heavy eyes met a goodness greater than darkness in seeing mauve meet wine on arced petals. As I traced spiny stems adorned with minuscule pink orchids, I outlined a beauty larger than my inner despair and discontent. Marveling in the playfulness of white polka dots on emerald leaves opened my eyes to the wonder that all of this, including me, was dreamed and breathed by a God I cannot see.

When the largeness of loss swells, and the knot in my chest becomes bars blocking me from hope, I study the order of small things. I stoop to the curve of petite petals, and in turning, they curve my soul—the magnificent grace of bending with the largeness in me to the glory I can see. Simone Weil writes that "the beauty of this world is Christ's tender smile for us coming through matter."[21] When the smile of God feels hidden behind clouds of

----

21 Simone Weil, *Waiting on God*, Routledge Revivals (New York: Routledge, 2009), 60.

pain, grief, and self-doubt, the beauty of this world pulses with the energy of its Maker, whispering for us to come see.

Awareness of my emotional state brought me there. Noticing and naming my darkness compelled me to give it space to dwell alongside beauty and light. Holding both within view brought my eyes back to the grace that God's presence and power sustain everything.

Cross the threshold into the place of your pain. Recognize the ground. Embrace the mystery of the place you find yourself. The cloud of suffering is a place we cannot understand, yet it is for our good. God never takes us there to torture us. And the cloud never stretches on forever, even though it feels like it might.

Within the transitional space of suffering, our communion with God is being formed and strengthened. Every adequate developmental relationship requires transitional space, where a child can learn how to explore and to be alone.[22] Suffering brings us to the transitional space in our relationship with God where we learn to trust and stand in who God is forming us into, our truest selves in Christ.[23]

With the cloud over the purpose of our pain, we stand in the reverberating truth of Job's words at the end of his long experience of suffering. Job realized he could not understand or define the hand of God in his pain. He said, "Surely I spoke about things I did

....

22 Jack O. Balswick, Pamela Ebstyne King, and Kevin S. Reimer, *The Reciprocating Self: Human Development in Theological Perspective* (Downers Grove, IL: InterVarsity Press, 2005), 75.

23 Balswick, King, and Reimer write, "The true self is the authentic, spontaneous self, aware and comfortable with his or her uniqueness. . . . Transitional space allows for the expression of the true self. The false self results from a lack of transitional space." Ibid., 76.

not understand, things too wondrous for me to know."[24] Instead, he worshiped.

In suffering's clouded place of mystery and worship, we are changed. In the place of mystery, pain becomes a passage.

Our suffering is the dying of an old world and the emergence of a new one. Out of chaos and cloud, God forms the stunning shape of our new hope and new world, our union with him. When we find ourselves in the fog, we stand where ordinary time and space become occupied by the coming King whose reign will never end. When we cross the threshold into the fog, we step into the thin space where this world—and our selves—are being healed by the coming of God's love.[25]

Walk into the barren, empty places of your pain, because this is where God will fill you with himself.[26] This liminal space is where we hate to go but where God is always leading us.[27] Don't run from what does not make sense or try to explain it away. Dissonance is the birthplace of all abiding Christian hope. Embrace mystery as the place God dwells. Embrace your suffering as the paradoxical place where you will be made whole.

"When we were children," Gerald May writes, "most of us were good friends with mystery. The world was full of it and we loved it. Then, as we grew older, we slowly accepted the indoctrination that mystery exists only to be solved. For many of us, mystery became an adversary; unknowing became a weakness."[28] We have to become like little children again, with all of their vulnerability and wonder, to see mystery as a place of possibility. These are the

....
24 Job 42:3.
25 N. T. Wright, *Surprised by Hope: Rethinking Heaven, the Resurrection, and the Mission of the Church* (New York: HarperOne, 2008), 259.
26 As Ruth Haley Barton writes, "We cannot escape the fact that willingness to walk into the empty places is a precursor to finding God." Ruth Haley Barton, *Invitation to Silence and Solitude* (Downers Grove, IL: InterVarsity Press, 2010), 88.
27 Rohr, "Grieving as Sacred Space," 22.
28 May, *Dark Night of the Soul,* 132–33.

ones Jesus said the kingdom of God belongs to—the little children with wonder in their eyes, looking at Jesus like he's a friend.[29] The cloud of suffering is a threshold you can cross, a place you can choose to occupy, a space where you become like a little child to be made whole. The cloud is where you learn: the kingdom of God belongs to you.

---

29 Mark 10:14.

CHAPTER 6

FULLY HUMAN

Jesus Joined Us on the Floor

> *The Savior assumed a body for Himself, in order*
> *that the body, being interwoven as it were with life,*
> *should no longer remain a mortal thing. . . . He put*
> *on a body, so that in the body he might find death*
> *and blot it out.*
>
> **—ATHANASIUS, *ON THE INCARNATION***

> *Only the suffering God can help.*
>
> **—DIETRICH BONHOEFFER, *LETTERS***
> **AND PAPERS FROM PRISON**

The year I got sick, I was a resident assistant tasked with emotionally and spiritually supporting a group of nearly thirty college women. I spent hours each day in the library writing papers, the day punctuated by meals and coffee dates with women from my dorm. After copious amounts of tea sipped between fervid research binges, I would walk across the dark, quiet campus to my hall, where I would stay up even later attending to the tears of peers getting over breakups or venting anger about their roommates.[1]

Suffering has an inelegant way of reversing relationships, and where I was used to being the comforter, I suddenly found myself learning the harder role of recipient. Out of nowhere the majority of my life consisted of crying tears of my own within the confines of four cinderblock walls, too sick on most days to even get out of bed. The body that had effortlessly carried me through the winding, steep paths of my mountainous college campus could now barely hold itself up in bed. The limbs that climbed limestone cliffs between classes now struggled to walk fourteen steps to the bathroom.

At night I often couldn't sleep because of pain, and after hours of no relief, I'd cry from the excruciation. One suitemate in particular would often find me awake in the middle of the night, weeping on the floor of our shared study room. Instead of turning the other way or quipping about how early she had to get up for an exam, Katie would join me on the floor, massaging my aching hands as I sobbed into her chest.

In the first half of my college experience, I had started to better learn the gospel story, where weakness is welcome and hurt is held. But I didn't know it yet in my limbs and ache and shame. I had to learn that on the floor, where Katie came to find me, willingly holding my weak body in her embrace. When I went to college, I signed up for an education of books and lectures. I didn't realize the education I would need for the rest of my life was the nearness of Christ and his body to the indignity, brokenness, and shame in my own.

....
1   A version of this story first appeared in *Fathom*. K.J. Ramsey, "The Education I Never Signed Up For," *Fathom* (September 11, 2018), *www.fathommag.com/stories/the-education-i-never-signed-up-for*.

This is grace: God joined us on the floor of this earth.

God did not stay far from our pain. He did not judge it from a distance. He did not pity it from the other side of the universe. He became it.

Grace is solidarity instead of scrutiny. This is the power that sustains us when suffering lingers.

God took on the human condition you and I so struggle to bear so we could be enfolded in his love. "Love consists in this: not that we loved God, but that he loved us and sent his Son to be the atoning sacrifice for our sins."[2]

Many of us are confused about the purpose of Christ's coming and the heart of our hope, often without realizing it, and the confusion amplifies our pain when suffering lingers. The very persistence of suffering might not fit with the hope we thought we had or the Jesus we thought we were serving.

We'll keep looking in the wrong places for grace in our suffering if we don't reexamine and rearticulate the substance of our hope and the message of our Lord.

Jesus said his Father's purpose in sending him to earth was for him to bring the kingdom of God near to us.[3] But our churches often collapse his message and our hope into salvation from sin. Many unintentionally reduce the gospel to a disembodied cure and moment of transformation, neglecting to give us the scaffolding of story and solidity of physical experience needed to build a life on God's promises. Jesus came "to seek and to save the lost,"[4] and he seeks and saves us into a new reality of experiencing his presence, memory, and story. We are saved not only *from* sin. We are saved *to*

....

2   1 John 4:10.
3   Mark 1:15; Luke 4:43.
4   Luke 19:10.

join and enjoy a kingdom where Christ reigns in love, is restoring all that has been broken by the curse of sin, and is personally present in and among us.[5]

In his coming, Jesus brought the kingdom of God near to us, so near that his Spirit now lives in us, comforting us and filling us with a presence that brings life. The kingdom of God is both our hope and the grace that carries us toward hope's fulfillment. It is a reality we take part in now, even as we continue to feel the heavy weight of brokenness.[6] Right now "the whole world lies in the power of the evil one."[7] But the Father "has rescued us from the domain of darkness and transferred us into the kingdom of the Son he loves."[8]

The future of God's good reign has already been set in motion with the resurrection and ascension of Jesus and the gift of his Spirit. Salvation is already here, but its fullness awaits Christ's second coming. The wholeness of our salvation is a guaranteed reality that sculpts our present existence. As New Testament scholar Gordon Fee writes, our present is shaped by "the singular reality that God's people belong to the future that has already come present. Marked by Christ's death and resurrection and identified as God's people by the gift of the Spirit, *they live the life of the future in the present,* determined by its values and perspective, *no matter what their present circumstances.*"[9]

....

5   I first heard this concept of "saved from" versus "saved to" in an undergraduate doctrine course at Covenant College with Dr. Kelly Kapic.

6   As citizens of the kingdom of God, we experience two conflicting realities. As theologian and pastoral counselor Eric Johnson writes, "Humanity is unknowingly under the degrading and enslaving influence of Satan (1 John 5:19), along with the 'powers and principalities' (Eph. 6:12), and the earth is now the site of a spiritual battle going on between Satan and his forces and God and his, ultimately limited by God's power and plan." If we fail to remember this, the bitterness of death will unnecessarily overpower the flavor of life Christ continuously offers us. Eric L. Johnson, *God and Soul Care: The Therapeutic Resources of the Christian Faith* (Downers Grove, IL: InterVarsity Press, 2017), 132.

7   1 John 5:19 ESV.

8   Col. 1:13.

9   Gordon D. Fee, *Paul's Letter to the Philippians* (Grand Rapids: Eerdmans, 1995), 50–51, emphasis added.

Christ has brought his kingdom near, and he will extend its fullness when he returns. The timing of his return is beyond our understanding,[10] but we wait now with a patience powered by the Spirit's presence and an eagerness to experience Christ's life even in the midst of death.

Rather than pining after some distant day when we will make it to heaven, we base our hope on the reality that Jesus is creating a new earth where those who are united to him will live, play, sing, and love with redeemed physical bodies in a redeemed physical world as a redeemed people united in worship and radiant in diversity.

Our hope is not in being beamed up to heaven upon death with suddenly perfected bodies. Our hope is informed and colored by John's vision in Revelation 21: the New Jerusalem comes *down* from heaven. Hope in suffering is never for a disembodied day when we can finally escape the bodies, relationships, and circumstances that have caused us so much pain. Biblical hope is expressed not in certainty but in curiosity, hearts that acknowledge and accept Jesus is already King, lives that look for the restoration of his rule right here, people propelled by a willingness to see Jesus turn every inch of creation from cursed to cured. The relationships that were broken will be made right; our relationship to our bodies, each other, the earth, and God will be fully and finally restored.

The kingdom is already and not yet; living in its tension rather than panicking for release is the only way to be pulled into the trajectory of hope.

Hope becomes tangible when we consider that through Christ's ascension, God's space and ours are no longer distant. As New Testament scholar and theologian N. T. Wright asserts, heaven and earth are not two separate places within the same continuum of time and space. Rather, Wright says, "they are two different dimensions

....
10 Matt. 24:36; Mark 13:32.

of God's good creation."[11] Because of the resurrection and ascension of Jesus, because we have been united to him by the Spirit, even while we wait for Jesus to return, we will experience God's space and life intersecting ours. And one day, Jesus will return wearing the scars of his suffering along with his royal robes, and when he does, he will unite heaven and earth forever.

In Jesus Christ suffering becomes the place where God came to find us. The chasm between the Father's love and our heartbreaking circumstances has been crossed because "the Word became flesh and dwelt among us."[12] Jesus, God-made-flesh, has stepped into the middle of the chasm, forever changing the expanse into a channel. In suffering, the space between heaven and earth can become thin, paradoxically placing us closer to the King's presence, power, and life. Pain can be a portal.

It is through suffering, not in spite of it, that God extends his reign and rule to the world he so loves. Truly, as Wright encourages, "the *method* of the kingdom will match the *message* of the kingdom. The kingdom will come as the church, energized by the Spirit, goes out into the world vulnerable, suffering, praising, praying, misunderstood, misjudged, vindicated, celebrating: always—as Paul puts it in one of his letters—bearing in the body the dying of Jesus so that the life of Jesus may also be displayed."[13]

To bear the death of Jesus in our bodies, we must recount his embodied life. Jesus came to walk where we walk, to see, to touch, to hold, to weep, and to heal. His embodied life changes everything

11 N. T. Wright, *Surprised by Hope: Rethinking Heaven, the Resurrection, and the Mission of the Church* (New York: HarperOne, 2008), 111.
12 John 1:14.
13 Wright, *Surprised by Hope*, 112.

about ours. Jesus' real body, his real trust, his real feelings, and his real agony create his real victory for us.

Jesus has a body.

Jesus' perfect faithfulness culminated in the sacrifice of his life. He carried the weight of all our brokenness to the cross—every failure, every abuse, every trauma, every disappointment, every genetic abnormality, every depressive episode, every curse, every speck of human selfishness. Jesus lifted every ounce of this world's heaving brokenness in his body until he could breathe no more. This is love on full display: Jesus allowed our brokenness to break him, and the breaking bought our life.

But his lungs rattling as his breath slowed to nothing and his spear-pierced side form but the consonants of his love. To hear the full sound of love's force, we must listen for the human vowels of Christ's story. Love leaped humanward from heaven, and it forever changed the sound of being alive.[14] If we jump straight to the climax of the cross and the resurrection, love won't reverberate through our every breath and bone. So listen, listen to the syllables of God's love.

Love entered the world set on suffering for us as one of us. Love came not in sparkling array, not in a form that would stop us on the street. Love entered the world like we all do, through the womb of a woman, as a crying, sticky infant in need of his mother's milk. Jesus did not plummet down from heaven into a thirty-three-year-old's body to carry our sin to Calvary.[15] Love came not as a swift, stealth infiltration mission but as a human being who would grow from a baby to a man. To hear the sound of God's love, we have to hear the sounds of being human. A Jesus who never screamed as a baby is

....

14 In the incarnation, we have what James Torrance describes as a "double movement of grace." This movement is both God-humanward and man-godward through the person of Jesus by the Holy Spirit. James B. Torrance, *Worship, Community and the Triune God of Grace* (Downers Grove, IL: InterVarsity Press, 1996), 32.

15 Kelly M. Kapic, *Embodied Hope: A Theological Meditation on Pain and Suffering* (Downers Grove, IL: InterVarsity Press, 2017), 89.

hard to receive as Lord when I am screaming in pain. A Jesus who never hungered is distant from the distress of those who do. This is not our God. This is not love. But Love, Jesus is.

It's so simple and scandalous, we could miss the sound: in choosing to become human, God knew dependency. The sound of love comes in the dependency of a baby who needed to be fed, wiped, and soothed. Saint John Chysostom wrote in the fifth century, "The Ancient of Days has become an infant. He who sits upon the sublime and heavenly throne now lies in a manger. . . . He who has broken the bonds of sinners is now bound by an infant's bands."[16] I wonder if we struggle to hear the sound of God's love because we have been listening for the sublime instead of cries. It's a body that brings God's love to us.

Jesus' body carries his story. His body speaks. Remembering Jesus lived in a body amplifies his story to a volume loud enough to hear as our own. As we consider the real, embodied life of Christ, we can encounter him with imaginative hope of how his humanity is recreating ours. As theologian Julie Canlis encourages in her lovely book *A Theology of the Ordinary*, when we look at the life of Jesus, we can continually ask, what is Christ doing to my humanity here?[17]

Without realizing it, "we often think of the Incarnation as the warm-up to the real drama," writes systematic theologian Oliver Crisp. "Jesus needed to become human so he could die for us. What many Christians have forgotten is that our redemption began with the Incarnation."[18] It is Jesus' willingness to be born, to be dependent, to be embodied that forms the substance of our faith. The cross has to carry something. Jesus' real body is what forms our real hope.

....

16 Saint John Chrysostom, "The Mystery," in *Watch for the Light: Readings for Advent and Christmas* (Maryknoll, NY: Orbis Books, 2008), 232.
17 Julie Canlis, *A Theology of the Ordinary* (Wenatchee, WA: Godspeed, 2017), 30.
18 Oliver Crisp, "By His Birth We Are Healed: Our Redemption, It Turns Out, Began Long before Calvary," *Christianity Today* 56, no. 3 (March 1, 2012): 31.

Hope is not found in a far-off Jesus but in the God who was willingly born as a baby, learned to walk and talk, frustrated his parents, felt the heat of the sun, and knew the pain of misunderstanding. Luke tells us that as a boy, Jesus "grew up and became strong, filled with wisdom, and God's grace was on him"[19] and that he "increased in wisdom and stature, and in favor with God and with people."[20] Jesus experienced human development like we all do. His faithfulness included growing up.

Jesus was not just inhabiting a physical body long enough to be killed on a cross, after which he could go back to being Light of Light. He was not God in disguise. He was not acting at being human. We know this, but I'm not sure we believe it in our bones enough to hold it in our hurt. Something about God being human enough to have diarrhea just doesn't sit well with our Sunday-school-trained sensibilities.

If I cannot allow Jesus to be as human as me, then I cannot allow him to be Lord. He hands me redemption from nail-pierced hands and speaks life with lips that cried out in anguish. My faith is only as real as I believe his body to be. As I consider this reality that I would have blushed at or been corrected for as a kid in church, Jesus becomes real enough to make my broken body his home.

"God, who cannot get sick, who cannot grow hungry, who cannot bleed, who cannot die—*this* God comes near so that the impossible becomes possible," Kelly Kapic reminds us.[21] The seemingly impossible task of enduring suffering *and* rejoicing in it is born in the impossible reality that God became human. The implausibility of having joy in a body with an incurable disease is made possible by God in a body. The possibility of hope in *your* despair is alive, here, as close as your breath.

Because of Jesus, the sound of love is human. Its echo is no

19 Luke 2:40.
20 Luke 2:52.
21 Kapic, *Embodied Hope*, 89.

farther than the thrum of your heartbeat, the sobs of your spouse, or the gurgling of your stomach. If we separate Christ's work from his physicality, we will undervalue the substance through which he chose to redeem the world. Love came in a body like mine and like yours. I cannot worship what I would like to ignore. To hold love in my heart, I have to honor Christ's body by valuing my own. The healing of our brokenness comes through the cross first in Jesus' willingness to live an embodied, human life. The whole of our redemption is found in the whole of his life. Joy and love are forever bound in skin and bones.

Jesus had to trust his Father.

Questions dangle in the closet of my heart, hanging as the clothing of my mistrust. I reach in without realizing, grasping for a rain jacket to protect me from being soaked through by suffering. The pain that keeps falling from the sky makes me want to stay inside or at least well-covered. Somehow, even though my mind knows God didn't cause my body to create an internal civil war between my immune system and my body's native tissues, my soul still isn't sure. My mind knows, as Tim Keller writes, that "God will allow evil only to the degree it brings about the very opposite of what it intends."[22] But my heart sinks in what feels like an existential abyss. I want to cover myself from God because the storms I fear he's sent are wiping me away like a flash flood, eroding roots that felt secure. Branches that blossomed fall and are swept away. The storms of suffering can make me feel like a tree stripped of leaves. No fruit. A withering vestige of former vitality.

Suffering can erode our trust in God. I think it also rebuilds

....
22 Timothy Keller, *Walking with God through Pain and Suffering* (New York: Penguin, 2013), 284.

it. But first suffering kills the god I thought I was worshiping so I can know the God who is actually here. In his book *The God-Shaped Brain*, psychiatrist Timothy Jennings discusses a study done by Baylor University researchers who found that only 23 percent of Americans view God as benevolent or loving, while 72 percent have a fear-based view of God. Further, Jennings describes research that demonstrates worshiping a God of love stimulates the brain to heal and grow.[23] Jennings argues that worshiping a God of love is what shapes our brain to be healthy and whole, which I agree with entirely, but we can't scrunch our face, hope really hard, and open our eyes to believing in a God who is love when we've spent a lifetime accustomed to believing God might be punishing us. This is the central, critical reversal of suffering in faith. Will I allow suffering to strip away the angry god I fear but want to love so that I can encounter the God who loves me through my fear?

Jesus' life offers the power we need to let ourselves be loved.[24] Where you and I reach for jackets of self-protection, Jesus offers the clothing of his own lived trust in his Father. Just as the sound of love is physical, the clothing of trust is the material of Jesus' real faith lived out in real time and space. Mistrust lives in a hidden closet full of coats in my heart, but God is renovating my heart, giving me the new clothing of his Son. I cannot form trust on my own, and neither can you. But this is grace: the coming of Christ "is not only the coming of God as God, but it is also the coming of God as man to do vicariously for us what we cannot adequately do for ourselves."[25]

Our lasting clothing of trust was woven and sewn in the lived experience of Jesus walking this earth. Somehow we think that

23 Timothy R. Jennings, *The God-Shaped Brain: How Changing Your View of God Transforms Your Life* (Downers Grove, IL: InterVarsity Press, 2013), 27.
24 And, phew, being loved by God does not look like what we want or think we need, but, hallelujah, it is good.
25 James B. Torrance, "The Vicarious Humanity of Christ," in *The Incarnation*, ed. T. F. Torrance (Edinburgh: Handsel, 1981), 144.

because Jesus was God, his work and trust must have come easy, as though he could snap his fingers to do all he wanted. By focusing on his deity, we've forgotten his humanity, and in forgetting his humanity, we've lost sight of the footsteps that can guide us to hope. Jesus "emptied himself by assuming the form of a servant, taking on the likeness of humanity."[26] To save us, Jesus became us. Fully human. My Lord, your Lord, had to trust his Father every hour of his life.

Jesus had to depend on the Father to do everything. He had to trust the Father's heart to carry him forward, and walking forward meant walking toward death. In chapter 5 of John's gospel, we read about Jesus healing a man who had been disabled for thirty-eight years. We're told the Jews persecuted Jesus after this because he was healing on the Sabbath. Jesus told the Jews he was working on the Sabbath because "my Father is still working, and I am working also."[27] Then he says, "Truly I tell you, the Son is not able to do anything on his own, but only what he sees the Father doing."[28] His response rings like a bell, waking me up to the actuality that Jesus Christ knows what it is to be utterly dependent on God to guide, fill, and empower his work.

Further, Jesus identified the Father's love for him as the power filling everything he did. He tells the Jews, "Whatever the Father does, the Son likewise does these things. *For the Father loves the Son* and shows him everything he is doing, and he will show him greater works than these so that you will be amazed."[29] In this passage, we're told the Jews had started trying even harder to kill Jesus for calling God his Father. This is a hostile, threatening conversation, and as a human, Jesus' real physical body had to be coursing with cortisol, just as ours would. He felt the stress. His chest had to

....
26 Phil. 2:7.
27 John 5:17.
28 John 5:19.
29 John 15:19–20, emphasis added.

be tight with alarm, his heart beating fast in the presence of those who wanted him dead. The physical reality of a body in danger makes his response astounding. Jesus' response to judgment and palpable stress was to tell the truth about his relationship with the Father. In the face of threat, Jesus told the true story of who he was—loved by the Father—and what his purpose was—to do the Father's work of giving life to the dead.

There, among people who hated him, who judged him as disrupting their community of faith, in circumstances that were more tense than we can imagine simply reading words on a page, Jesus stood secure because he knew his Father loved him. He persisted in doing his Father's work, because he knew his Father's love was true and with him, and later he declared, "The one who sent me is with me. He has not left me alone, because I always do what pleases him."[30] If I am busy shielding myself from harm or trying to answer the question of evil, I could miss this: Jesus had to have faith. And the foundation of his faith was his relationship with his Father. Jesus confessed to those who hated him his Father's love was the center of his bold work in the world, the center of his purpose, and the center of his trust. Jesus found his security in the Father alone.

The faith of someone impermeable to stress means nothing to me. I can't take Jesus' faith as mine if I don't think he really had to believe. I can't wear the coat of his trust if I think his trust came easy. I can't experience the crouching dependency of my suffering as the prostration of prayer without beholding Jesus as needy—needing his Father's love, reliant on him for every breath, looking to him for guidance and strength. Jesus' neediness might offend our theological sensibilities. It might make us squirm. But it also might help us treat our own needs as prayers that are heard. Our Lord is no stranger to the painful dependency we feel so intimately in suffering. In Jesus, our needs find communion. In him, reliance was

30 John 8:29.

not shame; it was grace. As I behold Jesus' real trust in his Father, the storms of suffering don't diminish me. Jesus' human trust in God in his life, which was full of stress and suffering, makes me more fully human in mine. His trust creates the possibility of ours.

Jesus has emotions.

Where sanitized religion tries to desaturate the influence of emotions by demonizing them as parts of ourselves we above all cannot trust, Jesus shows us feeling.[31] Jesus lived affected by life, by human suffering, and by love. We often picture him as static and placid. We picture him wrong. The pastor and theologian B. B. Warfield wrote in 1912, "It belongs to the truth of our Lord's humanity, that he was subject to all sinless human emotions."[32] Love did not come to us unaffected, even though we might picture perfection as a continuously happy countenance or an always-firm handle on life. Just as our emotions are the energy moving us through life, Jesus' emotions guided his work. We cannot separate our redemption from his emotion. The part of ourselves we are often most uncomfortable with was the energy that moved Jesus in the work of our redemption.

Warfield and other scholars have said that the emotion we see most frequently in Jesus in the gospels is compassion.[33] Throughout the gospels we see him especially moved to compassion by people experiencing physical suffering and pain.[34] Jesus was moved by what others might ignore. He didn't consider those who were suffering an impediment to his work or a frustrating detour from the

31 Remember, in chapter 4 we discussed how our emotions reflect God's.
32 B. B. Warfield, "On the Emotional Life of Our Lord," in *The Person and Work of Christ* (Philadelphia: Presbyterian and Reformed, 1950), 93.
33 See Warfield, "On the Emotional Life of Our Lord," and Stephen Voorwinde, *Jesus' Emotions in the Fourth Gospel: Human or Divine?* (London: T&T Clark, 2005) and *Jesus' Emotions in the Gospels* (London: T&T Clark, 2011).
34 Kapic, *Embodied Hope*, 83.

thing he'd rather be doing but the heart and summary of his mission. He said, "The Spirit of the Lord is on me, because he has anointed me to preach good news to the poor. He has sent me to proclaim release to the captives and recovery of sight to the blind, to set free the oppressed, to proclaim the year of the Lord's favor."[35]

While working on this book, I stayed briefly at a monastery where one afternoon the guest master mused, "I think every person in the Bible Jesus healed is a snapshot of him." To think that God saw himself in those whom society casts aside makes me reconsider my value as one who doesn't earn much, who can't always fully participate in life, whose suffering often feels like an inconvenience and an obstacle. I wonder if the blind men, the woman who bled for twelve years, the man with a shriveled hand, the demon-possessed, the deaf, and the lepers were each a snapshot of my Lord. Can we tolerate a God who identifies himself with the weak? The frequency of Christ's compassion toward the suffering must change the way we see our weakness.

Jesus was moved by love, and his love included anger. He turned over the tables of the money changers in the temple, furious at the way people were treating his Father's house. Just before he healed the man with a shriveled hand, Jesus became angry at the religious people watching him for caring more about following rules and being right than about the suffering person right in front of them.[36] In Matthew 23 he spoke with a sharpness far from any peaceful image we have of him, repeating six times, "Woe to you, scribes and Pharisees, hypocrites!" He called them fit for hell, whitewashed tombs, blind guides, and snakes! Jesus used words of force, and if we had seen him, we would have felt his fury.

Christ's faithfulness included anger. In Mark 10 people were bringing their children to be blessed by Jesus, and he was indignant at the disciples for keeping the children from him. Warfield called

....
35 Luke 4:18-19.
36 Mark 3:5.

his anger here annoyance or irritation.[37] Jesus got irritated. Anyone who has ongoing pain knows irritation is sometimes unavoidable when you are hurting, and to hear even Jesus felt irritation is a surprising relief. Faithfulness in suffering can and must include anger.

Jesus' anger not only validates ours but also shows anger can be an energy that manifests God's glory. When Jesus heard his friend Lazarus was sick, he said, "This sickness will not end in death but is for the glory of God, so that the Son of God may be glorified through it."[38] He waited to go visit his sick friend, even though waiting meant Lazarus would die before his arrival. We're told Jesus was deeply moved in his spirit when he stood before his friend's grave.[39] The Greek word translated as "deeply moved" can also be translated as "anger" or even "rage."[40] Kapic writes, "As he faced the sights, sounds, and smells of grief and death—the culmination of physical suffering—he was angry at the destruction caused in the world by the entrance of evil. Jesus' tears grow out of this rage, and he weeps."[41] He raised Lazarus from the dead, but first he wept. His glory is shown through tears rising from anger. Jesus gave a foretaste of his coming resurrection, and the flavor included the stench of death and the salt of tears. Jesus said Lazarus' sickness was for the glory of God, and that glory came through rage-filled tears. Love sounds like Jesus weeping.

Holiness can look only like Jesus. It will sound like crying, like groaning. It will speak with force, with fury. It will include peace and gentleness, but it will never be stoic. Wholeness is God filled and moved by feeling. The Light of the World shines in a malleable, tender heart. Suffering arouses difficult emotions. We need not judge them as diametrical to the heart of our Savior.

....

37 Kapic cites Warfield in *Embodied Hope*, 83.
38 John 11:4.
39 John 11:33, 38.
40 Kapic, *Embodied Hope*, 84.
41 Ibid.

Jesus knows pain.

Jesus, through whom each galaxy was formed, every ocean filled, and each petal of every flower imagined, creates new life through his obedient suffering. His experience of genuine physical, relational, and mental pain re-creates our own.

We become whole, we become truly human, because Jesus lived a whole, human life including pain. Jesus knew the pain of betrayal and the sting of denial. Throughout his entire life he felt the loneliness of being misunderstood by those closest to him. His own family called him crazy.[42] Even his brothers did not believe in him.[43] He felt the grief of being judged by his religious community, who saw him as an imposter, a rebel, and a threat to kill. And when Jesus shared with his disciples about his coming suffering and death, Peter rebuked him, chiding Jesus, totally missing the truth of what he had shared.[44] How frustrated Christ must have felt to hold his coming agony in his heart alone. God, who in himself is community, chose to feel and know the ache of loneliness.

As Jesus walked toward the cross to give himself entirely for us, he wrestled with the turmoil of accepting suffering in a human body made for life. Preparing for death, he withdrew with some of his closest disciples to pray. Jesus pleaded with his Father to take the cup of suffering from him: "My Father, if it is possible, let this cup pass from me. Yet not as I will, but as you will."[45]

Jesus, the maker of the night sky, pleaded under the stars for suffering to be taken from him. Jesus—fully human and fully God—asked not once but three times for his suffering to pass.

....

42 Mark 3:21.
43 John 7:5.
44 Matt. 16:21-23.
45 Matt. 26:39.

Even Jesus wanted relief. Even Jesus felt the inner battle of living in a body made for love in a world where faithfulness requires bearing pain.[46] He felt anguish so profoundly, his sweat was like drops of blood.[47] The German systematic theologian Jürgen Moltmann writes that this chapter in the Luther Bible is headed "The Struggle in Gethsemane," and he says it was Jesus' struggle with God.[48] Jesus' pain included struggling with God. Because of Jesus, faithfulness *includes* struggling with God.

Just a stone's throw away, his closest friends in the world couldn't even stay awake to pray with him in his hour of greatest need. Jesus knew the utter isolation of suffering, the harrowing place it takes us where others cannot or will not go. His pain included struggling alone when he felt his deepest anguish.

In the quiet of the garden, with the disciples asleep while he was in agony and the light of the moon his only earthly company, Jesus sweat over suffering, spoke his struggle to his Father, and in being heard felt the Father's love. Of his prayer of anguish, Dietrich Bonhoeffer writes, "He knows that the cup will pass by his accepting the suffering. Only by bearing the suffering will he overcome and conquer it."[49]

In the first garden of history, the first human beings rejected what they were given in favor of what they wanted. In the garden of Gethsemane, Jesus accepted what we couldn't to create the willingness we need. Our will is awakened by his willingness to die.

A garden held our original sin, and a garden held the faithful human response to God that spreads the seeds of Christ's life into our bodies, broken by the curse and flailing to be free. Jesus' agony

46 Eric L. Johnson, *God and Soul Care: The Therapeutic Resources of the Christian Faith* (Downers Grove, IL: InterVarsity Press, 2017), 253.
47 Luke 22:44.
48 Jürgen Moltmann, "Prisoner of Hope," in *Bread and Wine: Readings for Lent and Easter* (Maryknoll, NY: Orbis, 2014), 148.
49 Dietrich Bonhoeffer, *Discipleship* (Minneapolis, MN: Fortress, 2015), 55.

and trust in the garden cultivates our lives into a garden that will never stop producing fruit.[50]

What I didn't know in my earliest days of suffering, what I forget even now in despair, is that Jesus knows my pain more intimately than I do. The Light of the World is the Man of Sorrows. God, the Creator of everything, was despised. God, who has always been and always will be, felt rejection. He knows what it is to be sick and to suffer. He knows the shame of being considered worthless. He didn't merely identify himself with those who suffer. He became one who suffers. His pain was genuine, and it included the suffering of the entire world. For "he himself bore our sicknesses, and he carried our pains."[51] He bore my disease, and he carried my pain. He bore your greatest grief and largest loss, carrying them to a place we wouldn't and couldn't.

Our hope rises in Christ's willingness to carry what we hate and did not choose. Our darkness becomes light when we see his sacrifice included holding our suffering in his body, a mystery beyond our comprehension, an incomprehensibility that makes his love tangible. It was weight he chose and felt. It was as real as the weight of this book in your hands. Jesus carried my suffering, and he carried yours, all the way to the place we could never take it.

Jesus cosmically carried all our suffering in his body to the cross. His faithful human suffering reversed the curse of Eve's grasping for a wisdom bigger than her body could hold. He accepted what was given. He wanted the wisdom revealed in the tree, the resolution of good and evil that only his body could hold.

"Because no other could do it," Simone Weil writes, "he himself went to the greatest possible distance, the infinite distance. This infinite distance between God and God, this supreme tearing apart, this incomparable agony, this marvel of love, is the crucifixion."[52]

....
50 Rev. 22:1-2.
51 Isa. 53:4.
52 Simone Weil, "The Love of God and Affliction," in *Simone Weil: Essential Writ-*

When we are united to Christ, our suffering can be music that reverberates with the sound of his love. His love crosses the universe, echoing into the darkest, deepest silence of our suffering, enfolding our pain into his song of infinity-crossing love.[53]

In Jesus, "God stands in solidarity with the world and takes responsibility for the evil and suffering in the world," writes disability theologian John Swinton.[54] Before God brings life from death, he stands in solidarity with our suffering in the human Jesus Christ. In experiencing pain, by feeling the force of brokenness in his body and soul, Jesus became the greatest comforter we can ever know. "We do not have a high priest who is unable to sympathize with our weaknesses, but one who has been tempted in every way as we are, yet without sin."[55] Advice or consolation from someone whose life has been easy isn't that comforting or welcome. Jesus has earned the right to be heard. Christ's love can resound in our hearts because he has known the pain we carry. He has known the pain of the whole world.

The incarnation of Jesus Christ is God's radical declaration that human bodies matter. The life, suffering, and death of Jesus is God's patient insistence that suffering and ordinary, embodied life are places of grace. The resurrection of Jesus is God's affirmation that all matter matters.[56] God called his creation good, called our bodies very good, and he insists on enfolding what he made into a life that will last.

....
ings, ed. Eric O. Springsted (Maryknoll, NY: Orbis, 1998), 46.
53 Ibid., 53.
54 John Swinton, Raging with Compassion: Pastoral Responses to the Problem of Evil (London: SCM, 2018), 87.
55 Heb. 4:15.
56 As Barbara Brown Taylor writes, "The resurrection of the dead is the radical insistence that matter matters to God." Barbara Brown Taylor, An Altar in the World: A Geography of Faith (New York: HarperOne, 2010), 62.

This is grace: God joined us on the floor of this earth in the person of Jesus and forever changed the abyss into a portal. In the faithful life of Jesus and in the Spirit's raising him from the grave, we can anticipate and even taste our liberation.[57] His life changes how we can live our entire, embodied lives. Suffering can become the point at which we find ourselves nailed to the center of God's heart and rising with his breath to walk in the world reborn.[58]

....

57 Miroslav Volf, *The End of Memory: Remembering Rightly in a Violent World* (Grand Rapids: Eerdmans, 2006), 113.

58 Simone Weil writes, "The man whose soul remains oriented toward God while a nail is driven through it finds himself nailed to the very center of the universe; the true center, which is not in the middle, which is not in space and time, a totally other dimension, the nail has pierced through the whole of creation. . . . In this marvelous dimension, without leaving the time and place to which the body is bound, the soul can traverse the whole of space and time and come into the actual presence of God. It is at the point of intersection between creation and Creator. This point is the point of intersection of the two branches of the Cross." Weil, "Love of God and Affliction," 55.

CHAPTER 7

BEAUTIFUL UNION

Christ's Life Becomes Our Own

Christ takes on the whole of our lives so that we may partake of the whole of his life.

—CHRISTIAN KETTLER, *THE GOD WHO REJOICES*

Deep, buried beneath all you feel
and all the lines of your story
that are twisted, tangled knots
is

a subterranean self—you,
hidden with Christ in God,
and

a subterranean story—you,
knit into the story where
all that is deep, buried,
twisted, and tangled
is

soil of a growing goodness
that will last.

Jesus came close to bring us close, to enfold us back into the love for which we were created. In him we participate in a new reality and a grand story. We hold a living hope. Yet if you are like me, sometimes you don't know how to derive comfort from Christ's story. With depression that isn't lifting or pain that's still present, God can feel more absent than near. Sometimes the sheer volume of suffering in our stories makes it hard to see how we could be participating in a story bigger and better than pain, a story that won't end in defeat.

Our neural networks tend to reinforce the story that suffering is a barren desert, and we'll continue to experience it as such unless we encounter another person standing there with us. We cannot make sense of our stories on our own. Attachment researchers measure the extent to which an adult has made sense of their life story, through a tool called the Adult Attachment Interview.[1] Those who have a coherent grasp of their life story have what is called secure attachment. Secure attachment is reflected and expressed in an integrated prefrontal cortex, a mind and life like a tree planted by streams of water.[2] Later in this chapter, we'll learn more about having an integrated prefrontal cortex and moving toward secure attachment, or as Paul describes, being "transformed by the renewing of your mind."[3]

We didn't become withered trees with eroded roots on our own. Our patterns of relating often become insecure through inadequate formative relationships with our caregivers early in life and through traumatic experiences even into adulthood (perhaps including the suffering that led you to pick up this book). This is why we might believe God is good but feel he is cruel. Without secure attachment, we will struggle to make sense of our stories, including our suffering, and our minds will continue to stay knotted, disintegrated, and discouraged.

....

1   George C. Kaplan and Mary Main, "Adult Attachment Interview" (unpublished manuscript, 3rd ed., Department of Psychology, University of California, Berkeley, 1996).

2   Ps. 1:3.

3   Rom. 12:2.

We don't become rooted, fruitful trees by thinking harder. As psychiatrist Bessel van der Kolk has commented about trauma, this is not "something you figure out. This is about your body, your organism, having been reset to interpret the world as a terrifying place and yourself as being unsafe."[4] Many of us have come to experience our suffering as scorched earth, our bodies as betrayers, and God as negligent, even if our churchy goodness makes us afraid to admit it.

We can only develop the capacity to make sense of our stories and renew our minds to greater wholeness through encountering an outside relationship. The field of psychology describes this process as earned secure attachment.[5] Theology describes it as union with Christ. God is inviting us into a paradox of great possibility. Becoming whole in and through suffering requires experiencing the presence, power, and story of the Person we most fear has abandoned and neglected us—God himself.

Our suffering only makes sense alongside the story of the risen, reigning Christ. Suffering roars with lies about who we are. *Forgotten. Forsaken. Unloved.* When suffering lingers, we'll only hear the sound of love and the harmony of hope in the rhythm of Christ's breath, which is nearer than you might expect.

In Jesus we have been united with a presence, memory, and story that touches and transforms our stories of sorrow into stories of life. In Christ the suffering we want to escape becomes the place of more fully participating in the reality of the kingdom of God. Our union with Christ does not rescue us from our earthy existence. Rather it plants our feet on the arid soil of suffering and makes it fertile ground.

We can only experience stories including suffering and

....
4   Bessel van der Kolk, "How Trauma Lodges in the Body," interview with Krista Tippett, *On Being*, March 9, 2017, podcast audio, *https://onbeing.org/programs/bessel-van-der-kolk-how-trauma-lodges-in-the-body/.*
5   Curt Thompson, *Anatomy of the Soul: Surprising Connections between Neuroscience and Spiritual Practices That Can Transform Your Life and Relationships* (Carol Stream, IL: Tyndale, 2010), 136.

prolonged waiting as good by encountering the story and person of Jesus, not once but over and over in the myriad moments when life leaves us breathless, bereaved, or bored. Remembering Jesus' entire, embodied life changes how we live our entire, embodied lives. The presence, memory, and story of Jesus can and will re-member us into people who know they are loved.

Remembering Christ and being re-membered by him is not simply a matter of recounting his story but of reexperiencing his life in the most mundane and maddening moments of our lives. Our memory, our stories, and the vast neural networks propelling us toward either health or death must all be touched by the presence, memory, and story of the only man who died but still lives.

⚓

Jesus does what we could never do for ourselves. The curse of sin has woven every human life into a rope that will hang us. Every human story is braided into the hanging weight of shame. We fight for air, gulping, gasping, and flailing. Each of us, aware of our imminent death or not, fights for a life we cannot secure.

Christ came to release us from our kicking, futile attempts at escaping death's knot by cutting the gnarled loop wrapped tight around our flesh, to hold us, exhausted on the ground of our execu-tion, and with the breath that raised him from the dead, to breathe life into our broken bodies so tenderly, so completely, and so con-tinuously that we can walk with him again.

How close Christ came forms the reality of how close we can come; his life unites us to God. Jesus came as one of us, in a body marked by death's cords. God came in a body that could get sick, a body that would be scorned and spit at, a body that would die. And a body that would live. It was as a human that Jesus faithfully offered himself as a living sacrifice to breathe God's breath of life into our bodies suspended and subject to the power of death.

Jesus' life is not just an example. The thirty-three years he walked the dusty ground of Israel were not simply a section of history recorded to encourage, challenge, or confuse us. No, in Jesus the new power and new reality of the kingdom of God intersects human history. The hanging noose of shame no longer has to be the end of the human story. The domain of darkness is no longer the only power at work in this world or your life.

The boundaries of your story are no longer the dates of your birth and death.[6] Every mundane and monumental moment of Christ's life was lived to bring before the Father the faithful human response to God's love we could never produce on our own. Each unrecorded kindness to strangers and his family, every moment of simple or searing trust, his thirty years of living in obscurity before beginning his ministry—Jesus' humanity is the foundation and force of our human faith. By the Spirit, the breath of God, Christ's faithful life becomes ours, here and now, in the places we most struggle to be faithful and faith-filled.

There is more at work within, between, behind, and before us than the disappointments or drudgery of today seem to indicate. Jesus' life enfolds our stories in a story larger than our own, of a people more loved than we realize, a power beyond our perception, and a world more lasting than we can imagine. The life of Christ is ours to receive, a life lived on our behalf that turns our fainthearted faith into worship. Jesus does in us what we can never do for ourselves.

Suffering feels like the narrator of your story, telling a tale of woe. But Love is its true Author, writing your life into a larger story of a people pursued, oppression obliterated, death defeated, and a world reborn. The reign of God and your enjoyment of it is the reality that will last.

....
6   Eugene H. Peterson, *A Long Obedience in the Same Direction: Discipleship in an Instant Society* (Downers Grove, IL: InterVarsity Press, 2000), 170.

To say we struggle to experience that reality now, as we suffer, is probably the greatest understatement of this book. Our struggle is more than a matter of belief or its absence, and learning to recognize and tend to its origins will gradually change our experience.

Because of how God designed our brains to function, our stories shape how we experience the world, including how we experience the story and presence of Christ. We might believe the fact that God is loving, but our memories often have molded us to experience him as anything but. Psychology and neuroscience teach us that how we experience the present is constantly being shaped by our past. Memory is forming the substance of our stories, but most of us are unaware of its steering.[7]

While we think of memory as a collection of autobiographical facts, it is actually a complex function of how the brain processes each moment, situation, and relationship and directs our response. Our neural structures are formed through our early relational experiences, which attachment researchers call our "internal working model."[8] Our minds are etched with the ways we have experienced others and responded to them, and this constitutes, on a deeper-than-conscious level, how we continue to experience our relationships with others, ourselves, and God.[9] Your past shapes your present and your future.

In 1949 the Canadian psychologist Donald Hebb described a concept that underlines why memory so powerfully shapes our lives: neurons that fire together wire together.[10] Every experience

7   The following section draws from the insights of Curt Thompson in *Anatomy of the Soul*, 65–78.

8   John Bowlby, *Attachment and Loss*, vol. 1, *Attachment* (New York: Basic, 1982).

9   Eric Johnson, *God and Soul Care: The Therapeutic Resources of the Christian Faith* (Downers Grove, IL: InterVarsity Press, 2017), 65.

10 Hebb was likely the first to propose this concept, but the phrase appears to be

you have corresponds with a specific pattern of neural networks firing, and each time you repeat an experience or behavior, the same set of neural networks fires. The more frequently a pattern is fired, the more easily it will fire in the same way in the future. Now known as Hebb's axiom, this concept demonstrates how our experiences carve well-worn pathways in our brains that reinforce and repeat similar patterns of doing, being, and believing.

Two of the most general forms of memory constantly sculpting our neural pathways are implicit and explicit memory. Grasping a broad sense of both may help you consider what is shaping your story and how that story can change.

Implicit memory is our most primitive form of memory, functioning even at birth and involving the lower regions of the brain (including the limbic system, brain stem, amygdala, and other regions of the right hemisphere). This type of memory stores, encodes, and retrieves experiences without our conscious awareness. Whether we are pouring a cup of coffee or walking down a street or perceiving the emotional atmosphere of a conversation, our minds automatically circumvent the circuitry needed for conscious, voluntary mental activity. Our bodies remember the way Dad got angry when we cried as kids, and it automatically associates the expression of vulnerability with a negative response, so much so that we expect anger or dismissal when we let our tears be seen by those closest to us now. Implicit memory makes simple actions effortless, but it makes mistrust and self-protection in moments when they are no longer needed effortless as well.

Our bodies remember our experiences without our conscious awareness, a fact that holds profound power for understanding and changing how we live. We often are experiencing something connected to and deeply influenced by our past, without being aware

first used by Carla Shatz in 1992. See Donald Hebb, *The Organization of Behavior: A Neuropsychological Theory* (New York: J. Wiley, 1949). See also Carla J. Shatz, "The Developing Brain," *Scientific American* 267, no. 3 (1992): 60–67.

of it. By paying attention to our bodies and how they are reacting to a situation, we can begin placing our current emotions and reactions into the context of our story. With kindness and curiosity, our bodies can be guides to places in our past that hold hurt and anxiety, pain far deeper than whatever we are experiencing now, wounds that need the tender care of Christ. Remembering that implicit memory is continuously directing the way we respond to our lives gives us room to live differently, to fire distinct neural networks, to create new pathways of peace.

Explicit memory is the form of memory we most commonly associate with remembering, including both autobiographical memory (remembering your birthday) and factual memory (remembering when a bill is due). Explicit memory starts developing later than implicit memory, at about eighteen to twenty-four months, as the hippocampus begins its work of integrating different aspects of implicit memory—feelings, perceptions, sensations, and bodily and spatial awareness. The hippocampus connects implicit and explicit memory, enabling our ability to recall and to know we are remembering. Our autobiographical memory emerges as our prefrontal cortex develops and integrates with the hippocampus, giving us a sense of self over time, understood through language and thought. Autobiographical memory gives us a sense of what we have lived, what we are experiencing now, and how the future may unfold. Explicit memory requires conscious attention and is what enables us to form a sense of story.

Implicit and explicit memory work in concert to shape our story, and it is through the lens of our stories that we view everything and everyone, including God and ourselves. What you have lived actively and constantly sculpts what you continue to live into. Remembering your story, down to the emotional tenor of your youngest years, places your hands in Christ's around your present to sculpt your life into the shape of his love. Instead of being subconsciously steered by unresolved pain, tending to the wounds in your memory can sculpt your life into the shape of God's love.

Our memory can obstruct both our view of God and the embodied reality with which we can experience grace, guiding us to view our ordinary bodies and ordinary days as prisons and deserts far removed from God and grace. Our stories can block us from grace when unacknowledged and forgotten, but when remembered with respect and care, they reveal the fingerprints of Christ's incarnation in our lives.

The chasm between who God says he is and who we experience him to be, especially when hard things keep happening, is not crossed by whipping our minds into submission with more theological facts or quickly naming suffering a gift.[11] This chasm is crossed only by new experiences, a relationship that forms love so deeply in our memory that acceptance and grace become our expectation.

In Jesus, we are continuously offered the relationship that will change our stories by renewing our minds, down to the very firing of our neural networks. We respond to our circumstances and God through the matrix of our emotional memory, and "emotion memories can be modified only through new emotional experiences."[12] Significant change in how we experience our circumstances—change in the memory structures of the brain that are reciprocally guided and shaped by emotion and relationship—is possible through "months and years of daily doses of loving communion with God."[13] Because Christ came, because he suffered, because he lives in us now by his Spirit, he is always crossing the chasm to us. In those experiences in which our memory has taught us to expect judgment and abandonment, he offers his presence.

....

11 Curt Thompson discusses this at length as well. See chapter 8 of *Anatomy of the Soul,* "Earned Secure Attachment: Pointing to the New Creation."
12 Johnson, *God and Soul Care,* 175.
13 Ibid., 66.

I wonder if we don't absorb the Breath of God swirling around us in suffering, loss, and seasons of monotony because we consider the story of Jesus as though it were a book whose only chapters that matter are the first and the last. We think of Christ like we think of ourselves—as though his bodily existence was simply a vehicle to accomplishing success. We unintentionally treat his body and our own as either commodities that will purchase happiness or inconveniences that will block it. I know we don't mean to. It's like exhaling the cultural air we breathe—so automatic that we aren't aware we are doing it.

The entire, embodied life of Christ forms the food of our faith, the nourishment that strengthens weakened knees so they can stand firm and tired hands so they can hold hope. But we prefer the rich diet of a Christmas feast followed by Easter dessert. We heap holiday food on the plates of our minds, plates coated in the acidic film of prolonged pain, and we wonder why we feel foggy and faint. In Christ's entire life—including his birth, anonymity, ministry, suffering, death, and resurrection—we encounter the faithfulness that can nourish our often-feeble faith into strength. We long for joy, and it is here. Christ's entire life can fuel our entire lives, down to our very breath. Joy becomes the habit of our hearts, the energy directing our minds, and the truth upholding our bodies when we encounter our ordinary lives as the place where Christ is present. The middle of the story you are in is the place where God is already meeting you, merging your life with his own, and establishing his kingdom of death-defying love.

Your present discomfort has to bond with Christ's past faithfulness to create future hope. Today, in tears or trouble or exhaustion, your present suffering can be the place where you experience Christ's faithful endurance of suffering. Even your hopelessness can be a prompt to trust the endless well of hope Christ has on your behalf. Your present pain can marry Christ's past faithfulness, re-forming your memory into the contours of his love. A memory reshaped is a future reimagined.

For Jesus' entire, embodied life to transform our entire, embodied lives, we have to allow his love to rule every part of who we are. Living under the loving lordship of Christ requires paying attention to our bodies and stories with an alertness that produces "love, joy, peace, patience, kindness, goodness, faithfulness, gentleness, and self-control."[14] The fruit of the Spirit is a mind and life guided by grace and flowing with love. The fruit of the Spirit is a well-integrated prefrontal cortex (PFC).

The PFC is the part of the brain that creates and sustains many aspects of our well-being, including our ability to make sense of our story and shape its trajectory. The neurons in this part of the brain generally require conscious attention to activate, a challenge for us all. To remember our story and live into the better one where Christ has already come near, we have to pay attention.

Psychiatrist Dan Siegel describes nine functions of living that strongly depend on the PFC.

1. *Body regulation.* The PFC helps us regulate our heart rate, breathing, and digestion when we are facing stress. It receives information from our nervous system and can influence how we respond to situations that are triggering our fight-flight-or-freeze impulse.
2. *Attunement.* The PFC allows us to consider what another person may be thinking or feeling and shift our internal state in light of it. It allows us to resonate with, ponder, and respond to people's internal worlds, including our own.
3. *Emotional balance.* The PFC helps regulate our emotions so

14 Gal. 5:22–23.

that they are a rich part of our lives yet do not constantly overwhelm us.

4. *Response flexibility.* The PFC helps us pause before responding, creating space between what our bodies sense and feel and how we choose to act.

5. *Empathy.* The PFC creates capacity to feel what another is feeling, while remaining grounded and aware of oneself. It allows us to perceive how another person is seeing the world.

6. *Insight.* The PFC enables us to consider our past and future in connection to the present, giving us the ability to make sense of our stories.

7. *Fear modulation.* We often feel fear when facing situations similar to ones that have frightened us in the past. The PFC can calm the limbic system and amygdala, inhibiting our fear so it does not override our thoughts and behavior.

8. *Intuition.* The PFC enables us to recognize and interpret sensations from throughout our bodies, especially from the viscera (heart, lungs, and gastrointestinal tract). It opens us to the wisdom of our bodies, which helps us sense the world around us and our safety and place in it.

9. *Morality.* The PFC empowers the ability to consider not only our own good but the good of others, overriding immediate impulses so we can sense the meaning of experiences and challenges and seek the welfare of others.[15]

The PFC is the part of our brain we most need to gain awareness of our story and live into the trajectory of hope. Without outside intervention and intention, death and decay knot our minds into pathways and patterns of disconnection and disintegration. When facing the burden of suffering on our own, we will disconnect and

....
15 Daniel J. Siegel, *Mindsight: The New Science of Personal Transformation* (New York: Bantam, 2011), 26–30.

detach from our own minds and from one another.[16] All of life is a battle for our attention, and suffering strongly suggests we close our eyes and lock our hearts.

The prolonged, continual experience of weakness, pain, and loss will frequently place us in a position that feels vulnerable and unsteady. Stress, uncertainty, and difficulties will continue to bombard our bodies, putting us into fight-flight-or-freeze mode and triggering a deluge of overwhelming emotion. But there is a power at work within us, greater than the barrage of suffering. There are always two roads before us: the lower road, where our brain becomes unbalanced, the PFC and its regulating functions become temporarily disintegrated, and the lower regions of our brain take over, shoving us down a rockslide of fear and disconnection; and the higher road, where the distress of suffering reminds us to pay attention to ourselves with care and seek security in the One whose brain is always balanced and whose heart is always kind.[17]

We'll often stumble down the lower road, but Jesus goes with us, ready and willing to help us rise. Even when our brains are flooded and we are flailing, "we have the mind of Christ."[18] When we stand in the soil of suffering, abiding in the One who stood firm in suffering before us, this world touches the next, and we are slowly changed from the inside out. Suffering is a place we now find ourselves in, and it is the place where we can experience how near Christ has brought his kingdom.

....

16 Thompson, *Anatomy of the Soul*, 170.

17 To help you practice finding security in the One whose brain is always balanced and whose heart is always kind, I recommend reading Curt Thompson's *Anatomy of the Soul* and carefully walking through each of the exercises he includes throughout the book. Another excellent resource for learning how to relate to yourself and God from a place of security is *Boundaries for Your Soul* by Alison Cook and Kimberly Miller (Nashville: Thomas Nelson, 2018). I also cannot more strongly recommend seeking the help of a trained therapist, counselor, or spiritual director. Everyone needs the help of a counselor at some point in their life. To seek counseling is not weakness; rather, it is a courageous response to the God who valued your life enough to die for you. Seeking help will be worth the effort.

18 1 Cor. 2:16.

Suffering does not have to be a barrier to the renewal of our minds. It can be the rocky footing that reminds us to reach for the God who already came to the ground.

In Christ we encounter a human faithfulness we could never muster—a faithful trust in God that stands in our stead, gives us strength, and carries us farther into the story of redemption. Our lives now exceed the bounds of time, space, and our memories because Jesus has intersected time and space with his life and reign. He does in us what we can never do on our own.

Our stories are no longer confined to our years, constrained by the cords of death. Our potential is no longer fueled by privilege or extinguished by its lack. Our memories are now united with Christ's memory; every moment of his trust, obedience, persever-ance, and joy is now mysteriously and authentically ours to access and apply.[19] He has faith when we have none. He has trust when ours is thin.[20]

Christ is taking all that was cursed and is re-creating it as blessed. By inhabiting the place of the curse and inhabiting it now in us by his Spirit, Christ is redeeming every inch of scorched earth through our stories finding their home in his.

By being born, Christ affirmed the body as the place where God

....

19 Martin Luther writes, "This is the principal thing and the principal treasure in every Gospel. Christ must above all things become our own and we become his. . . . The Gospel does not merely teach about the history of Christ. No, it enables all who believe it to receive it as their own, which is the way the Gospel operates." Martin Luther, "Sermon for Christmas Day: Luke 2:1-14," in *The Sermons of Martin Luther* (Minneapolis, MN: Lutherans in All Lands, 1906), 1521-22.
20 Theologian Christian Kettler writes, "Jesus believes when I am unable to believe. Jesus acts when I am unable to act. Jesus loves when I am unable to love. Jesus forgives when I am unable to forgive. Jesus lives when I am dead in my sins. That is the power of truth become personal, the power of a vicarious life." Christian Kettler, *The God Who Believes: Faith, Doubt, and the Vicarious Humanity of Christ* (Eugene, OR: Cascade, 2005), 102.

is present. By growing up, he established obedience to the slow, painful work of maturity and development, showing us slow growth is sacred. As Scottish theologian T. F. Torrance points out, when Luke tells us that "Jesus increased in wisdom and stature,"[21] he is using a Greek word that describes Christ's growth as a struggle, perhaps more accurately translated as "he had to beat his way forward by blows."[22] Jesus' obedience included his submission to the ordinary, painful way we humans have to develop, learn, and grow, and it included battling the genuine human nature he assumed into willing obedience to God's will. We want to be whole without work, but even Jesus had to grow in wisdom in invisible, repetitious, mundane ways to curve human nature back to God's will.[23]

Our lives have been knit into the history of the entire people of God, including Jesus, and as we present our bodies as a sacrifice and meeting place with Christ, love slowly becomes our language and orienting reality. In Christ our lives are pulled into a reality greater than death and decay, a faithfulness that infuses the dirt of our suffering with the breath of life. A Christian is a person whose life has been expanded, whose memory has been extended thousands of years beyond their own, and whose present is enveloped by the presence of Love. Whether we feel or recognize it, even in suffering—especially in suffering—God intersects our lives with his presence, and his presence is always enfolding us farther into the reality of his certain, steadfast kingdom of love.

This was Jesus' mission: "to take to Himself and reclaim ('assume') every aspect of ordinary human life and turn it back to the Father as a place for communion."[24] In his body, in his trust, in

....
21 Luke 2:52.
22 T. F. Torrance, *Incarnation: The Person and Life of Christ* (Downers Grove, IL: InterVarsity Press, 2015), 64.
23 The best, most succinct treatment I have found on the humanity of Christ and its import for our ordinary lives is Julie Canlis' small book *A Theology of the Ordinary* (Wenatchee, WA: Godspeed, 2017). I'm indebted to her wisdom, especially in this section.
24 Canlis, *A Theology of the Ordinary*, 30.

his emotion, in his pain, he is taking every aspect of being human and turning it to the Father to be held by his love. In our bodies, in our trust, in our emotions, in our pain, Christ is reviving every atom of humanness that was broken by the fall. We participate in the life of the world to come, then, not simply by pining after suffering's eradication but by abiding in Christ in our weakness every time our feet hit rocky ground.

Today I woke with a groan, those first morning movements—the tilt of the head, the shift of fingers under cotton sheets—an immediate screech of pain. Usually it fades to a quiet drone, but today it's as thunderous as the steaming water filling my bathtub, where I stand, drawing my fourth bath of the week to relieve pain at an hour when most adults are midway through their morning's work. Stepping into the glimmering blue water, with the iridescent outline of bubbles cratered under the faucet, I hope the heat will hold the weight of my frustration. I'm choosing gentleness, but I'd rather not be in pain at all. I'd rather not be here at all.

I run a washcloth under cold water to cool my flushed, sweating face. Holding it there, cold drops stream down into hot tears. Is this a taste of Christ's blood-like sweat in the garden of Gethsemane? Could the agony of pain, my small, solitary pain in a bathtub in a bungalow somehow fill up what is lacking in his suffering? As the cool water mingles with my tears, my suffering mingles with the suffering of Christ. In the garden, he pleaded for the cup to pass—oh, how much I'd love for this cyclical part of my story to cease—but he trusted his Father's will. For the joy set before him, for the love that would enfold me and you into his relationship with the Father and Spirit, he said, "Not what I will, but what you will."[25]

....
25 Mark 14:36.

And as the steam settles in this small bathroom, and pain presses farther into my day, his trust becomes mine. I dry off, knowing grace will meet me, whether in bed or at my desk, in work or in rest, in acceptance of pain or in its relief.

Alone, I'd wallow. I'd hide *forsaken* in my heart like an inmate, counting the days God has left the child he supposedly loves be limited and lame. Doesn't wallowing often seem easier than remembering?

But I'm not alone; we're not alone. Christ's agony and trust infuse mine with a potency I lack. And as I remember him, these hard moments tingle with recognition. I have been united with Christ. He is present. Here. Now.

Your suffering may not drive you to a bathtub several times a week to relieve physical pain. It might not limit your ability to work, or maybe it does. But your suffering probably carries the same shrill cry of agony and the temptation to give up on God as mine. Your suffering probably haunts you with anger and sadness for all the wrong you seem to disproportionately carry. Your suffering probably repeats the pattern of fear-to-faith in more days and hours than you'd like, enfolding you in a dependence that can both dissolve and develop joy.

In the place of your weakness, Jesus stands secure in the Father's love for you. In the circumstances and memories that drive us to doubt, Jesus never wavers in remembering we are loved by God. And when we allow our tears, agony, and desire for relief to remind us of his, we are filled with Christ's memory of God's faithfulness. In moments when doubt could lead us down a dark road, sharing our grief with the Savior who willingly suffered fills us with faith to trust again. It's grace for the moment, grace to rise. Grace that holds us together like bubbles on bathwater, a beauty formed in tension rather than its absence.

In our mundane, repetitive moments of suffering, Christ's memory of living faithfully, of trusting the Father, of being loved, can be formed in us, turning stories that include suffering into stories of communion.

Suffering does not have to be a barrier. It can be a continual reminder that there is no part of your life where Christ is not present. There is no place too low for him to stoop. There is no part of your body too inconvenient for him to love. There is no place in your memory too dark for him to hold. There is no weakness too recurring for Christ to care for. He is patient, and he is present. Christ is holding us together by the power of his Spirit, wrapping scarred hands securely around the most shattered pieces of our stories, carrying them with care because he chose to be shattered first, and placing them perfectly alongside his own into a mosaic of glory.

So may you have courage to pay attention to him and to your life. May you have courage to join Christ in your place of weakness—as a place he is working and redeeming and filling with meaning—rather than trying to escape it, numb it, or name it as worthless. For in this place, he is present. In this, the place of your weakness, his power is perfected.

CHAPTER 8

PERSONAL PRESENCE

The Sacrament of Bearing Witness

Understand that your suffering is a task that, if handled correctly, with the help of others, will lead to enlargement, not diminishment.

—DAVID BROOKS, *THE SECOND MOUNTAIN*

The flame of individual faith weakens when it is alone, but in true community the fire of faith illumines the night.

—KELLY M. KAPIC, *EMBODIED HOPE*

The inconvenient but hopeful truth is that no one can enfold their life into the story of God redeeming all things without other Christians telling and witnessing their story with them. None of us can dwell in the tension of the narrative of redemption without others holding that tension with us.

We cannot keep paying attention to our lives and the life of God within them without others willingly witnessing our weakness.

The burden of suffering is too great. The pain of loss is too staggering. The very mechanisms of our bodies that sustain hope and create meaning cannot function in isolation.[1]

We can't write our stories into the story of wholeness without others writing it with us.

The tacit message in our churches, culture, and relationships is this: success is public; suffering is private. We see so little of each other's insides that we come to believe we might be the only ones suffering. We hide our wounds behind bandages of our own making while wondering if the hard things lingering in our lives somehow delineate between who belongs in God's family and who doesn't. Hiding and hurting, we become divorced from hope and detached from joy.

There is a better way to make Christ's story our own.

In the first years of my illness, I longed to meet one other person who was young and sick. I dreamed of meeting someone whose life looked like mine, who knew the discomfort of being at the age of peak possibility and potential energy in a body marked instead by fatigue and finitude. Nowhere did the space between me and others seem so wide than in my rheumatologist's waiting room.

In the last week were you able to:
Dress yourself, including tying shoelaces and doing buttons?
Get in and out of bed?
Lift a full cup or glass to your mouth?
Walk outdoors on flat ground?
Wash and dry your entire body?
Bend down to pick up clothing off the floor?

1   Curt Thompson, *Anatomy of the Soul: Surprising Connections between Neuroscience and Spiritual Practices That Can Transform Your Life and Relationships* (Carol Stream, IL: Tyndale, 2010), 112.

With the clipboard balanced on my knee, I slowly checked off the litany of reasons my life was different from my peers. My ears were perked to hear my name called by the kind nurse with the bushy, fading red hair—the one moment I would feel I was supposed to be there. With each glance around me, I noticed how clearly I didn't belong. In a room full of bodies adorned with canes, walkers, and gray hair, I felt simultaneously out of place and tethered to a future of sagging skin and twisted fingers. The pale blue walls and cushy chairs were a parody of comfort when the truth was sitting in that room felt like accelerated aging.

More than what I saw was what I did not see. I didn't see anyone who looked like me.

At some point it became easier to believe I was the only young person I knew who was suffering than to hold the pain of my life looking so different from my peers and so contrary to my expectations. Some people get to enjoy their lives, and others get to suffer.

I swallowed the story that suffering was my own private problem in a waiting room others were blessed to avoid. The lie went down easily, sliding through my neural network of lived experience that taught me uniqueness was the path to protection. I felt safe by judging others as blessed and myself as cursed, an odd way to push people away before they could reject me. I was pitiable, but I was special. I was suffering, and I both envied and judged those who weren't.[2] Like a drug, isolation brought temporary relief, but it could never satiate my longing or stabilize my hope.

We don't know how to name the darkness, so we use it to divide. In a culture that loves pleasantries but hates pain, we don't like acknowledging the way we sometimes feel overcome by doubt,

---

2   Again, bless my pretentious heart.

anxiety, and sadness. We swallow the darkness, hiding our hurt inside, but a seed swallowed rather than sown suffocates. The weakness we hide ends up separating us all from the hope we share.

I grew up barely knowing how to name and share the things most burdening me. As a church youth group regular, I spent many Wednesday evenings partaking in popcorn prayer, where we would awkwardly take turns asking God for help or telling him how great he is. Usually we would share prayer requests before starting. Often, one of us would share an unspoken request, which inevitably meant we wanted prayer for something we felt we couldn't or shouldn't share. We hid our hurts behind the word *unspoken*.

In those awkward youth group prayers, I missed the truth that difficulties are not something to hide but realities to name and endure. In denying hard things words, I missed learning that suffering is an expected part of being God's child and that sharing it is where hope will rise. Something unspoken can't be known. It becomes a private asphyxiation, a seed stuck in the throat of an individual body straining for the oxygen of God's love.

⚓

By the end of 2012 my life had again receded to the privacy of my home after another massive flare of disease. The inflammation in my spine and throughout my body had so ravaged me that I could barely rise from the couch where I spent most of my waking hours. Just a couple months before that I was thriving, crafting marketing copy, emails, and curriculum about social justice for the Chalmers Center, a Christian nonprofit doing incredible work. Suddenly the luster of dreams had dimmed into questioning whether I would ever be able to work again.

I compared myself with my able-bodied peers and coworkers and wondered why they could work when I could barely walk. I felt a strain between my inner potential and outer capacity, as though my body were wringing out all that was good in me into a lifeless heap on the couch. I had spent life differentiating myself from others; from my comments in classrooms to the way I dressed, my life was unknowingly built along the boundary lines of being unique. Now I was unique again for the reason I hated most—being a twenty-four-year-old who was too sick to work. Most days I couldn't leave the house, even for church, and in isolation I started sinking farther into the lonely story of being uncommonly afflicted.

There's a certain sadness to being alone most of the time because your husband is working extra hours to make up a sliver of the income you lost from being too weak. There's a certain defeat to watching filth accumulate around the tiny home you are confined to, because you are too sick to stand long enough to scrub half-eaten food off a pot. When you can't even keep your home marginally clean, it's almost too embarrassing to allow someone inside. Sarah came anyway.

She'd stop by once or twice a week on her way home from work, often knocking at the door without even calling first. Sometimes I considered hiding in the back room. Yet somehow I would rise from the dungeon of the couch and hobble my way to the door, those dozen steps a gulf to either sudden shame or stunning hope. Somehow, in the squalor and shame of disease, I found the courage to let her in. And somehow she kept coming. I'm still not sure who was more courageous. Sarah would sit by my side on my pleather, overstuffed couch and never mention the smell coming from my dirty kitchen.

Suffering had confined me to my home and reinforced a wall around my soul of safety in uniqueness—even dark, twisted, unwanted uniqueness. The wall was a facade that crumbled in Sarah's consistent presence.

She entered the place of my confinement, the prison of my perceived uniqueness, and sat with a willingness to witness the desperation I felt. I don't remember many of our conversations in those months. But I do remember weeping in her arms. I remember being allowed to be broken and hopeless. I remember that somehow among my stinging tears, the darkness of shame began to recede beside the gentle light of Sarah's acceptance. The woman who sat by my side, who never judged my filth or weakness, who eventually would do my dishes and bring me meals, brought light by her willingness to sit beside my darkness.

In those months, with our life shattered again by sickness, while I was reeling alongside my husband with constant anxiety about our future, I started to encounter the mystery of joy in suffering by being held in the place where sorrow dwells.

Light walked past my defenses, entered my darkness, and let me weep.

Months later, while I was still crawling out of shame's shroud, Sarah invited me into her own suffering. I was relieved to realize—shocker—that I wasn't the only young person suffering. Sarah, luminescent in her work and in my life, had just returned home from a mental health scare, a story which is hers to tell. She needed company for the day, and since I still wasn't working, I was glad to force myself out of the house, glad to return to her a small bit of what she had given me.

We sat shiva for shame in the afternoon light, watching Harry Potter in *The Prisoner of Azkaban* push back the dementors with the beaming glow of remembering what is good, of remembering he is loved. Seated on Sarah's sage-green thrifted couch in bodies that had let us down, as women afraid of their brilliant potential flickering into darkness, we unknowingly created a dawn of hope simply by bearing witness to weakness instead of hiding in shame.

A year before, it had seemed easier to believe I was the only one suffering than to bear the weight of my uncertain future. I hid my pain inside and wore shame like a musty but warm coat, believing comfort probably wouldn't come from anyone but the God who had the power to heal me if he wanted. Shame had long sold me the story that no one would comfort me. In that narrative, my capacity to access grace extended only as far as my tolerance for stress, which is, admittedly, not very far.[3] It made the reach of grace the length of my arms. Thankfully, grace can reach farther and surprise us into receiving it.

The gospel offers a better story, read not only in black letters on white pages but in the bodies of believers, words made flesh in the places of our pain. The gospel plants the seeds of Christ's life in our souls in the sowing of shared tears and the wordless resonance that happens when one right brain communicates love to another. Grace rises and reaches in the space between us.

Many of us have swallowed the seeds of our sorrow most of our lives, thinking hope was the possession of the strong and acceptance was the result of being worthy, not weak. We often struggle to experience the story of redemption as ours, because we have not experienced others as accessible, responsive, and engaged when we are weak.[4] Our implicit memory of vulnerability and weakness is often linked with overwhelm, dismissal, and hurt, resulting in isolation. How did your parents or caregivers respond when you were upset as a child? How much room was there in your home for your tears and fears? How often were you responsible to comfort your parents for theirs? We all have been shaped by a story our parents unknowingly wrote for us.

We strain to experience God as with us and for us in our suffering because love is not simply a cognitive truth to assent to but a

....
3   Jeffrey Zimmerman and Marie-Nathalie Beaudoin, "Neurobiology for Your Narrative: How Brain Science Can Influence Narrative Work," *Journal of Systemic Therapies* 34, no. 2 (2015): 59–74.
4   Sue Johnson, *Created for Connection: The "Hold Me Tight" Guide for Christian Couples: Seven Conversations for a Lifetime of Love* (New York: Little, Brown and Co., 2016).

relationship to be reshaped by. Right knowledge of the gospel will never be enough to root the love of God in our souls and enfold our stories into the story of redemption. God is after our whole selves, sitting in the spot where our minds expect rejection, inviting us to new, embodied experiences to renew our minds and re-form our hope. God draws near to us, and he longs to do so by his Spirit through the presence of his people. He has not left us alone.

Suffering re-presents us to God and others to be shaped by a love that welcomes weakness. Sometimes it gashes and gnaws, because not everyone is ready to encounter weakness instead of fixing or judging it. Other times it terrifies but heals to let something hidden be seen. The welcome of weakness can be the most powerful exchange we'll experience this side of Jesus' return.

While I was wrestling with whether I would ever be able to work again, my husband felt pinned down by the boulder of our suffering. The helplessness of watching me get sicker alongside his powerlessness to produce a better life were slowly strangling him. I was the weak one, and Ryan felt the necessity to be strong. He sacrificed his dream of finishing seminary so we could live in a city where I could receive practical help from friends. Setting his career aside, Ryan worked a data entry job that was so boring, his supervisor advised employees to watch movies while working just to stay awake. At home, I was barely able to walk to the bathroom without help. While our friends were starting businesses and families, we seemed immobilized by my disease. We were exhausted, souls sprawled on the separate mats of our perpetual vulnerability, unsure how to keep wrestling our individual challenges, let alone stand with each other to step toward a future that appeared bleak.

We didn't realize we both were sick. We barely had categories for depression and trauma and the way suffering like ours can erode trust and hope. Sadness and fear stood between us, and eventually, in the desperation of not feeling supported by each other, we told a friend we wondered if Ryan was depressed.

"You should talk to Kevin Eames," he said. "He'll be able to help you understand what's going on."

Our friend shared that Kevin had struggled with depression, and since he was a psychology professor from the college we had graduated from, we instinctively trusted that he'd probably be a safe person with whom to share.

So we found ourselves on a couch, facing Kevin and his wife, Lisa, slowly describing the darkness that felt like an invisible opponent we could never beat. Kevin made coffee and handed us ceramic mugs steaming with the subtle fragrance of nuts and chocolate, and we settled into the comfort of the Eames' unhurried presence. Over the hours of that first night in their home, we shared our story of suffering, my disease, our losses, and the nameless numbness that was making Ryan feel like a shell of himself. They had nothing to gain by having us over but made room for us anyway, never once indicating discomfort with what we shared or mentioning how late it was getting.

I stared into the inky residue at the bottom of my earthen mug, wondering if darkness would ever stop being the baseline of our life. Kevin's voice grabbed me out of my Neitzsche nonsense, as he said firmly to Ryan, "If you *weren't* depressed, I'd be concerned."

Kevin named what he saw and normalized what he knew.

Ryan and I glanced at each other in surprise, forming half smiles of relief. Instead of fear, we both felt validated and somehow closer. Kevin and Lisa had listened to us as though we were the most important story they could ever hear, leaning in, asking questions, and responding with emotion. And in their warm attention, more space was formed between me and Ryan to welcome each other like we were being welcomed.

The Eames made space for us to tell the truth about our story, the raven, throbbing truth that makes a lot of people squirm and pull out their shiny platitude swords to fight back the darkness they fear. Over time we'd learn that Kevin and Lisa had so persistently named the darkness in their own lives that they could sit with enough patience and love to help you name the dark and light in yours.[5] Theirs was a presence that formed space in our souls to remember the bigger story surrounding our lives, not by fearing the darkness but by naming it together.

Weakness is where Christ's power is perfected.[6] We like thinking community forms around our strengths, but in Christ the wonder of wholeness is welded through shared weakness. Most of us wander through life disowning or hiding half of what we've lived, afraid that showing the dark will distance us from the light. But we can never be whole or wholly known without seeing and sharing both our strength and our weakness.

One irritating grace of suffering is that it makes it difficult to keep ignoring or hiding weakness. Its persistent presence can be the rudder that turns us toward the place we naturally avoid, the place we can be most known.

We whose suffering lingers are often forced to see and share the weakness within, placing us in a position to recognize, accept, and offer the very thing that ignites communion. Without ongoing suffering, it's easier to keep hiding behind hurry. But when life

....

5   The Eames' lives have more than slightly resembled Job's. Kevin had diabetes from early childhood on and fully expected to not live beyond age thirty. His first wife died soon into their marriage. Kevin and Lisa's third-born, Daniel, had a rare condition that made him unable to speak. Daniel died in 2013. Instead of pushing others out in anger, the Eames have always made space for anger and pain to become wonder. Kevin died while I was writing this book, and I am honored to include you in his and Lisa's legacy of love.
6   2 Cor. 12:9.

keeps erupting with pain and loss, weakness demands a response. Suffering demands a reaction from all who encounter it—despair, apathy, or hospitality. In exposing our weakness and need, prolonged suffering is like gravity, planting our feet on the ground of our vulnerability, demanding honesty about where we are. Suffering repeatedly asks us to sit where others may be too busy or fearful to pause—to take part in the exchange that most reflects the inner life of God.

In my weakness, I am positioned to experience the glory of communion. In all of our continuing weaknesses, we are continually repositioned to experience the exchange of vulnerability into love.

On our own, we resist repositioning. We scurry from vulnerability like mice in a cat's shadow. Shame is the silent narrator of our old selves, the invisible puppeteer dancing our lives into dim corners. The story of shame is always working to disrupt the flow of energy in our minds, to divide us from one another, and to isolate us from hope. You'll recall from the previous chapter that without outside intervention, our minds are tangled into pathways of disconnection and disintegration. Without Christ, we are fixed on the path of that old story, with minds set toward death. But the same Spirit who raised Jesus from the dead is living in us, bringing life where there was decay.[7] And we "know that we have passed from death to life because we love our brothers and sisters."[8] Love is the expression of our life, and yet it can feel like water to our oil, fleeting and fearsome to receive.

In Jesus we are invited to a new relational reality, to put off the old self of hiding and withholding and to put on the new self of receiving and giving. Without new relational experiences, we'll habitually stumble down old paths to dark corners, stuck in

....
7   Rom. 8:6, 11.
8   1 John 3:14.

self-protection and scarcity. Because we live in the already and the not yet of God's kingdom, we already have the Spirit needed to walk in love but learning to walk takes time, and this ground will stay rocky until Christ returns. Because of this, our new relational reality will often feel uncomfortable, like being stretched.

Learning to inhabit our new selves—the life "hidden with Christ in God"[9]—will take time, will feel like losing control, and will require our attention. Though our old self has been crucified with Christ,[10] it will take time for our old brain to die.[11] The silent narrator of shame will keep whispering that safety is in the shadows, but in Christ we can listen to and respond to the voice of God's love calling us to light. The networks in our brains that shaped us to repel love and protect self may be accessible and operable until we die or Jesus returns. But death no longer rules us or our bodies, as much as it feels like it does. We must consider ourselves dead to sin—dead to the patterns and pathways that divide us from others, keep us in hiding, and enslave us to shame—and alive to God in Christ. We are alive to what does not come easy: "compassion, kindness, humility, gentleness, and patience, bearing with one another and forgiving one another."[12]

The shape of our new life in Christ, the life suffering and death will never defeat, is formed and fortified by the posture we take toward relationships. Love won't come easy, and it often will feel like exposure. Love will look like weakness and sometimes feel like dying. A soul alive in Christ allows itself to be repositioned. The Spirit turns us toward the place our old self would naturally resist, and our consent will be the continual reversal that forms the love of Christ into our memories, our neural networks, our innermost being.

....

9 Col. 3:3.
10 Rom. 6:6.
11 Thompson, *Anatomy of the Soul*, 229.
12 Col. 3:12–13.

"In our minds," Curt Thompson teaches, "to be vulnerable is to sense the potential for danger."[13] Often, when we are on the edge of being known, of being loved, shame prompts feelings of vulnerability. The lower regions of our brains react swiftly to what seems unsafe, and when our focus of attention is on self-protection—and we often don't realize it is—we cannot connect.[14] We'll never inhabit our new identity in Christ by sheer force of will but by encountering and extending our vulnerability with people who are likewise seeking to be made whole. We are slowly changed each time we acknowledge our vulnerability and impulse to self-defend and instead respond to our need to be known. Relationships coiled our minds into pathways of disconnection, and relationships will be what God uses to resurrect pathways of love and peace. Vulnerability experienced, extended, and received will be the communion bread and wine that continues to convert our dying, fragile selves into the unending likeness of Christ.

When we open ourselves up to being known, we open our stories and selves to be changed. As we share our stories, including our weakness, losses, grief, and hopelessness, and we are heard, our minds can experience new integration and well-being. (Recall the nine attributes of an integrated prefrontal cortex on pages 149–50 that offer and reinforce well-being.) When we share our sorrow and are received the way Kevin and Lisa received me and Ryan, our memories of what it means to be vulnerable are gradually changed. The more we share our stories and are received with compassion, the more our brains are shaped to anticipate love instead of rejection. When we allow

13 Curt Thompson, *The Soul of Shame: Retelling the Stories We Believe about Ourselves* (Downers Grove, IL: InterVarsity Press, 2015), 118.
14 Daniel J. Siegel, *Mindsight: The New Science of Personal Transformation* (New York: Bantam, 2011), 21.

others to bear witness to our weakness, we learn to relate to ourselves with kindness and hope. When someone listens and validates us as we tell our story, they ignite a new way of considering our story—as valuable, worth hearing, worth telling, *worth living*.

The brain's mirror neuron system mediates an empathy we could not create or feel on our own. Operating across all five senses, mirror neurons cue us to the internal state of others. Through the brain's resonance circuits, we instinctively imitate others' behaviors and come to resonate with their feelings.[15] Dan Siegel describes how we come to "feel felt"[16] in the giving and receiving of our presence and stories, writing, "Through facial expressions and tones of voice, gestures and postures—some so fleeting they can be captured only on a sloweddown recording—we come to 'resonate' with one another. . . . We feel this resonance as a palpable sense of connection and aliveness. This is what happens when our minds meet."[17]

As we share our stories and experience the listener as trustworthy, our brains release oxytocin, which researcher Paul Zak describes as "the neurologic substrate for the Golden Rule: If you treat me well, in most cases my brain will motivate me to treat you well in return."[18] Oxytocin helps us move toward one another, to share our stories and allow ourselves to be mutually affected by them. The embodied, neurochemical exchange of sharing our stories allows others to enter them, to experience what psycholinguists call "transportation," when another person has emotionally stepped inside the world of the story they are hearing.[19] The experience of resonance, of being heard and felt, unearths emotion and memory hidden deep in your

15 Ibid., 59–63.

16 Siegel coined the phrase "feeling felt," which he uses throughout his work, as in *Mindsight*, 10.

17 Ibid.

18 Paul J. Zak, "Why Inspiring Stories Make Us React: The Neuroscience of Narrative" (February 2, 2015), National Center for Biotechnology Information, *www.ncbi.nlm.nih .gov/pmc/articles/PMC4445577/*. Article from *Cerebrum: The Dana Forum on Brain Science*, vol. 2015 (January–February 2015), provided by the Dana Foundation.

19 Ibid.

right hemisphere and lower brain. It exposes the parts of your mind that most need healing, allowing the integration of layers of neural structures and systems, creating new pathways that previously did not exist.[20] Being heard rewires your brain.

For this to happen, we have to shape our silence into sound. The seed of sorrow must be sown to grow new life. We can't swallow our discouragement and expect to sprout hope. We have to allow ourselves to speak aloud the suffering our culture says should stay private. We have to let ourselves be seen, our stories be heard, our weakness be witnessed. We have to let friends into our dirty homes and ourselves into the homes of people we might barely know, just because kindness and hope could be there to discover.

Suffering must be shared, witnessed, and heard to be experienced as the fertile soil of Christ's kingdom, the ground where God comes to find and remake us. The incarnation becomes our felt experience when we allow others to enter the world of our story. When we feel felt by another, over and over, the love of Christ becomes a truer reality in our lives, the emotional memory of our brains, and the expectation of our hearts.[21] We need the embodied experience of another's welcome to better know the welcome of God, to let his love reverberate through our entire being so thoroughly and continually that we can welcome every part of our stories as contributing notes in the most stunning song.

To be changed by love, we must be willing to cross the threshold of

20 Thompson, *Anatomy of the Soul*, 137–38.
21 Eric Johnson writes, "Empathic listening affirms the created goodness of the other by taking his or her emotions seriously and communicates that those emotions are meaningful—they signify values—even when they misrepresent *current* reality to some extent, because present emotional meaning often re-presents experiences from one's story." Eric Johnson, *God and Soul Care: The Therapeutic Resources of the Christian Faith* (Downers Grove, IL: InterVarsity Press, 2017), 447.

our vulnerability, both as the one suffering and as the one sharing in their grief. When we encounter another's suffering, we experience the vulnerability of being limited in the scope and scale of our capacity to assuage pain. Recently, Sarah told me something she learned while visiting me during that long disease flare. Being there was easier than she imagined or expected. Sarah said that for a while she struggled with visiting me in those cold, cloudy months, because she wasn't sure how to help me. She wanted to encourage me but wasn't sure what I needed or wanted. She recalled feeling anxious about coming over, wondering if there was anything she could bring or something she could do to help alleviate the pain and anguish I was feeling. Over time, as she kept showing up, she realized I didn't need her to anticipate or fulfill my needs; I just needed her presence. And in the end, it was much easier to give that than to nervously try to figure out what would make everything better.

Often the pain that makes us feel most stuck is not our suffering; it is experiencing distress in the presence of people who expect us to get better faster than we can. I don't need one more recommendation of a diet, essential oil, or book that might fix the agonizing pain I experience. Facing weakness without ameliorating it makes us anxious, even though most of us wouldn't like to admit this or become aware of how true it is. When we encounter weakness, we sense the nearly invisible reflection of the weakness we all carry or might someday experience, and it makes us desperate to assert the little power we think we possess to keep the glare from scorching our socially-acceptable lives.

People who are suffering don't need fixing. They need presence. We need to be encountered not as problems to fix but as people enduring meaningful stories through which we all can behold a better, truer light. When we encounter suffering in each other's strained faces, we stare our own fear of inadequacy in the face. When we show up anyway, we say with our bodies that experiencing suffering matters, that we each matter, not for how perfect we are but for existing.

The exchange of vulnerability into love requires a receptive rather than reactive presence. My husband once defined this in a sermon as forbearance: maintaining an anchored presence in order to receive another person as they are, rather than reacting or retreating, and to hold their story as sacred. Receptivity creates the atmosphere in which love can re-form our memories and hope. When we are receptive, Dan Siegel writes, the "muscles of the face and vocal cords relax, blood pressure and heart rate normalize, and we become more open to experiencing whatever the other person wants to express. A receptive state turns on the social engagement system that connects us to others."[22] Perhaps the best way we can develop forbearance and extend hope, then, is by paying closer attention to our bodies in the presence of pain and vulnerability— ours or someone else's. To connect, we need to be aware of our body state and pay attention to it so we can shift it toward calm.

Those who want to extend comfort would do well to first notice their own discomfort. The discomfort of witnessing someone else's weeping or hearing someone's hopelessness is natural and normal. Most of us have had little practice existing in these liminal spaces. Notice your discomfort by checking in with your body. Are your shoulders starting to feel tense? Do you feel like escaping? Are you crossing your arms while you listen, unconsciously protecting yourself from absorbing some of the suffering spewing your way? You can notice how your body is responding to the situation you are in, not to judge your discomfort but to shift from unintentionally distancing yourself from someone's pain to entering into it. To grieve with those who grieve,[23] you have to allow yourself to be affected by someone else's suffering instead of rushing to reduce the pain.

....
22 Siegel, *Mindsight*, 215.
23 Rom. 12:15.

Notice your physical tension and squeamishness, but also notice how quickly you want to say things like, "I understand," "It's going to be okay," and "At least it's not . . ." Our swift verbal responses to others' suffering betray an inadvertent, sweetly worded selfishness of reducing our own discomfort when we intended to reduce theirs. This doesn't mean you can't use words to respond to the pain you encounter. It means you have a responsibility to pay closer attention to the reason you use the words you do.

We who want to receive comfort must also notice *our* discomfort, surprising as that might sound, considering we feel all too aware of how hard things are. By noticing the sensations in our bellies, the flow of our breathing, the tightness of our muscles, and the shape of our posture, we can better sense how safe we feel to share. By slowing down our breathing or even taking a moment to collect ourselves privately, we can try engaging in conversations that previously may have felt too vulnerable.[24]

We won't encounter the whole gospel in our suffering unless we encounter one another in pain. Suffering becomes a sacrament when we acknowledge we each come with empty hands. Our hands can't dismantle the pain suffering brings. Perfectly worded prayers probably won't be able to peel back the darkness. Our lovingly prepared casseroles and pies don't carry healing powers. Facing each other's pain requires facing the fact that only God can heal disease, quell fear, and set captives free. While we wait, we together behold the mystery that in our fragile bodies Christ already dwells.

***

Our crosses are too heavy to hold on our own. Even Jesus needed help carrying his. Why would we expect ourselves and others to

---

24 And, of course, this is outside the context of relationships that have already proved themselves to be traumatic and abusive.

carry crosses alone, when not even our Savior did? The weight of our burdens will crush us if we try to stack it into a story by ourselves.

Letting others' hands come under the weight of our stories is the only way to allow this present weight to expand us to hold the "absolutely incomparable eternal weight of glory."[25] This is how "we do not give up"[26] while "we always carry the death of Jesus in our body, so that the life of Jesus may also be displayed in our body."[27] No one can weave their story into the story of God making all things new without others witnessing their story and remembering it as a true part of something bigger. No one can experience the shattered pieces of their life becoming essential parts of a mosaic of grace and glory without others naming the colors, applying adhesive, and envisioning the larger picture God is forming.

We simply can't always remember on our own that Jesus holds our lives in a bigger story. As Andrew Peterson writes, "We all forget from time to time, and so we need each other to tell us our stories. Sometimes a story is the only way back from the darkness."[28] When my own memory fails me, I need others to remind me what is true. As Dietrich Bonhoeffer writes, "Therefore, the Christian needs another Christian who speaks God's Word to him. He needs him again and again when he becomes uncertain and discouraged, for by himself he cannot help himself without belying the truth. He needs his brother man as a bearer and proclaimer of the divine word of salvation. He needs his brother solely because of Jesus Christ. The Christ in his own heart is weaker than the Christ in the word of his brother; his own heart is uncertain, his brother's is sure."[29]

When my faith is fragile, I need others to have faith on my

....

25 2 Cor. 4:17.

26 2 Cor. 4:16.

27 2 Cor. 4:10.

28 Andrew Peterson, *The Warden and the Wolf King* (Nashville: Rabbit Room, 2014), loc. 4599 of 8979, Kindle.

29 Dietrich Bonhoeffer, *Life Together* (New York: Harper and Brothers, 1954), 25.

behalf.[30] Faithlessness and doubt should never be shamed; they should be a reminder to us all that we are part of a body that needs every part to remember, breathe, and walk in the rhythms of grace. As Kelly Kapic writes, "One of the regular ways the body of Christ maintains its health, even as parts of the body are attacked with disease [or depression or any suffering], is for the other parts to carry some extra weight."[31]

So who is holding your story with you?[32]

Whose hands are you inviting to tenderly touch the wounded places in your life? Whom will you trust to see you so fully and consistently that they can see the faith at the core of who you are and remind you of it when your eyes only see darkness? No one person can do this for us, and in some seasons of our lives it will take great creativity and courage to seek and find people willing to hold some of the weight of our pain. If Christ loved you enough to die for you, will you not offer yourself the grace of being known?

You are worth being known, no matter how exhausted, defeated, or disappointed suffering and your life story have made you feel. The risk of being known and the challenge of seeking people who are safe and kind enough to hold your story with care will be worth the effort. At times it won't seem like it, but there will be people who listen. There will be people who love. And love will make space for hope.

When the burdens of our hearts are many, when the despair of the present moment makes us wonder if we can keep trying or keep

30 Kelly Kapic writes, "The saints *speak to God for us* when we struggle to believe and speak alone. Further, the saints are also called to *speak to us for God* when we seem unable to hear him on our own. Their prayers sustain our faith; their proclamation reignites our hope." Kelly M. Kapic, *Embodied Hope: A Theological Meditation on Pain and Suffering* (Downers Grove, IL: InterVarsity Press, 2017), 128.

31 Kapic, *Embodied Hope*, 126.

32 I came across this question a long time ago in a podcast interview of disability theologian John Swinton. While I've lost track of the interview, you can find more of Swinton's thoughts on how our memories are held in our relationships in *Dementia: Living in the Memories of God* (Grand Rapids: Eerdmans, 2012).

living, the community of faith can bring light into our darkness. To receive their light, sometimes we have to tell them how dark things have become. Like Henri Nouwen writes, "One very important way to befriend our sorrow is to take it out of its isolation, and share it with someone who can receive it."[33]

Sometimes you have to do what I did even this week: tell some of your friends you are struggling to hope on your own and ask them to offer their presence in a simple way to remind you of the truth that you are never forgotten nor forsaken. This week, that looked like asking for quick phone calls to pray together. Instead of wallowing under the weight of my present darkness, I listened to the voices of my friends, and the light started to feel real, true, and tangible again. Was I ashamed to tell them I felt that weak? Yes. But in naming and sharing the dark, I put myself in a position to receive grace that was farther and deeper than my arms could reach. When I am willing to share my weakness, I am willing to let grace rush under my tired arms until they are strengthened to lift in prayer on their own again.

⚓

In the presence of other Christians, people in whom Christ dwells, with the seed of sorrow not swallowed but revealed and planted in the dirt of our inability to save ourselves, we digest a better story. In kind faces, long conversations, and tears shed but not shamed, we absorb the nourishment our bodies most need to become the remade, redeemed, resplendent selves Christ bought.

Unless a seed falls to the ground, unless the shame of our old self dies, it remains by itself. But if it falls, if we relinquish control for connection, the seed of suffering eventually cracks open under

....
33 Henri J. M. Nouwen, *Here and Now: Living in the Spirit* (New York: Crossroad, 1994), 50.

the moisture of our tears and attention. From the rent edges of its hardened exterior, this seed—scorned for years by family, and most deeply by ourselves—sprouts a root of new life.

The fallow soil of our lonely disappointments and desperation, tilled, tended, and watered by tears, touch, and sight, becomes rich as spring earth, the freshly fertilized land of a sustained life. The seed of our sorrow—relinquished, sown, and cracked open— becomes another shoot of a greater Vine, the fruited plant of abiding in Christ.[34]

The person who sows sparingly will also reap sparingly. The person who sows generously, even the scattered seed of sorrow and weakness—not strength, not wealth—will reap generously. And God, the generous, attentive, patient Gardener, is able and willing to make grace overflow to those who sow, so that in every way, in every relinquished story, tear, and fear, those with empty hands will have everything they need to do the good work set before them. He provided the seed and its sustenance all along.[35]

This planting won't always feel pleasant. There's pain in the scattering of seed, in the breaking open of our old, dead self. But later the sowing and tilling and tending yield the peaceful fruit of righteousness to those who have embraced it.[36]

Our tender branches, upheld by the ancient Vine and supported by other stretching, spanning branches, are pruned in patience by the Gardener himself so they will bear fruit. Fruit bursting with sweetness from sorrow. Fruit that lasts. Fruit named love. The fruit of a new self that looks like Jesus, trusts him, and extends his love to a world that needs it.

....
34 John 15.
35 2 Corinthians 9.
36 Heb. 12:11.

CHAPTER 9

THE COMMUNION OF SAINTS

Bearing Witness in Our Worship

He can no longer have God for his Father,
Who has not the Church for his mother.

—CYPRIAN (AD 423), "THE TREATISES OF CYPRIAN"

We who are many are one body in Christ and
individually members of one another.

—ROMANS 12:5

Church is where I've felt most alone and most alive. Being in the space of worship places my soul in the center of the paradox of praise in a body holding pain. Others who suffer tell me the same: going to church can be incredibly painful and exquisitely beautiful when we are wrestling at the foot of the cross for the rest Jesus promised. On wooden pews or cloth-covered seats, among the bodies of gathered saints whose smiles and lifted hands seem to speak stories of gladness, a suffering body can feel like putty stretched and spread to the margins of the room.

How many times have I bawled in church? How sharply have

I felt the searing heat of unhealed pain when the gospel accounts of Jesus' healing ministry are read? How many times have I been asked by well-meaning Christians, "Have you prayed for healing?" as though in a decade of disease I've never thought to ask God to take away my pain?

How many times have my tears mingled with wonder that God chose to draw near to heal the divide I feel in myself from his love? How many times have my tears become prisms, liquid lenses of the mystery of the God who chose to suffer for love?

In the gathering of saints, the stakes of suffering seem high. What we believe collides with what we feel. We carry our unanswered questions and unrealized desires into the pews, where we encounter reactions and responses to suffering that can wound and divide or join and heal. I wonder how many people whose lives are lined by long-term suffering end up quietly leaving the church or barely coming at all, simply because being there is too painful.

A few years ago, I spoke with a friend who felt she couldn't come to church anymore. She was suffering with two debilitating autoimmune diseases and was on the brink of losing her marriage.

"I've come to the conclusion that God has nothing to do with our suffering," she admitted. "It's easier to believe that than to justify my experience."

I didn't judge her words then, and I don't now. I've uttered similar ones in moments of despair. In a world that can crush and confound us in a million ways, hers is an understandable conclusion.

But at church, in pain, my heart gets turned inside out. Does yours?

The pain I don't want crashes into the hope I long for. Maybe it's because sitting still for an hour or two makes my joints stiffen. Maybe it's because the anger that seems to live in a dark corner of my spleen occasionally surfaces at church like a drunk uncle at Christmas, ready to spew its most irrational objections and judgments at my more perky brothers and sisters. (Sometimes I think I might strangle the next person who looks at me with pity-eyes and asks, "Are you feeling better?") Under the mud of pain's irritability, I'm certain people are judging me for sitting through yet another song while everyone else stands. So I judge them back with a mostly-internal scowl. But really, the judgment I'm afraid to put into words is against God. If he is omnipotent, why am I suffering? If he loves me, why does he let me hurt? When the questions I normally hang in a closet in my soul get dumped onto a pew, I feel my emptiness. Sometimes I long to be filled.

Suffering can feel like being severed from joy, but sometimes the presence of pain in the place where I am meant to praise turns the coldest, darkest part of my heart inside out into a garment of love with a warmth only the desperate appreciate.

Suffering can be a thread that ties us together instead of a sword separating us from joy. We'll only experience it as such, however, if the local church tells the truth about the place she finds herself in God's story. Throughout this chapter, I'll challenge you to hold hope for the body of Christ, even as we name the ways she has unknowingly failed us. For when two or three are gathered, Jesus is present. Jesus, who knows and values our pain more than we do, is present in the midst of his gathered, corporate body. Our innate resolve will never be enough to sustain our faith when suffering lingers, but in the body we *will* find grace. And I long for you to experience grace that sustains.

Without the communion of saints in Christ, our memory makes love a faint outline, overshadowed by the flux of our daily disappointments and the rising of anxieties rooted in the past. Eugene Peterson was more right than he probably knew when he wrote, "But we need other experiences, the community of experience of brothers and sisters in the church, the centuries of experience provided by our biblical ancestors. A Christian who has David in his bones, Jeremiah in his bloodstream, Paul in his fingertips and Christ in his heart will know how much and how little value to put on his own momentary feelings and the experience of the past week."[1] Both the history of the people of God and the unfolding history of our committed life together now, gathered around Christ crucified and risen, shape our hearts and minds to dwell in a love more steadfast than all our shifting feelings.

We'll only live and tell our stories as good when we live and tell them in community.[2] And I ache to share this, because while I've tasted the goodness of the body of Christ, I still grieve from the vast ways she has hurt me.

I imagine you do too, that you've felt the stinging pain of judgment and the hushed agony of isolation. I imagine you have your own pile of cutting, insensitive comments from other Christians and your own silent storehouse of unseen or unanswered needs. Or maybe you haven't felt particularly hurt by other Christians or the church, but you've quietly wondered if your story is valued by them. Maybe you have questioned whether you are wanted in the church, sensing you are too troubled, too weak, too sick, too different, or too poor to be included.

The body of Christ holds both hurt and healing. To enfold our lives into God's story of redemption, we have to enfold our stories into Scripture's story of a people. And for many of us, this is a continuous act of great courage.

In the body of Christ is both our pain and our healing, and

---

1   Eugene H. Peterson, *A Long Obedience in the Same Direction: Discipleship in an Instant Society* (Downers Grove, IL: InterVarsity Press, 2000), 166–67.
2   There *are* seasons and reasons we sometimes cannot attend church services (trauma triggers, illnesses that keep you homebound, distance, and more). If this is your current season, please know there is grace for you. Relationships with other believers remain a gift and grace you need, even if you can't access that grace in the same way others can or that you have in the past.

in you is *her* healing. Even as you cannot enfold your life into the life of Christ without the presence of others, the church cannot remember her whole story without you. So within these pages, pause. Consider the possibility that a people holds your hope and you, in part, hold theirs.

I recently sat in a church service where a few people were invited to share stories of ways God had dramatically moved in their lives over the past several weeks. I listened while shifting in my seat, trying to keep my joints from screaming too loudly for me to participate in the service. As I reached into my purse to grab some Zofran to abate the nausea surging to the tip of my tongue, I heard the pastor say, "Tell us how God healed you."

Beaming with amazement, a young woman at the front shared her story of miraculous healing. She had suffered from chronic rhinitis for more than two years, and her struggle to breathe had become so troublesome she was scheduled to have surgery at the end of the month.

At the end of every service, this particular church has people available for prayer, as a space for being encouraged, listening to God, and following him in faith. The woman described that just two weeks before, she had gone forward for prayer for another issue entirely and was surprised by what happened. She had not even mentioned her breathing issues, but the person praying for her sensed that for quite some time something had been blocking her from being able to breathe and prayed for its removal.

The woman said she felt encouraged but didn't think anything more of the interaction until later in the week, when she realized she had been breathing easily even with the spring pollen levels at an all-time high. By the next week her breathing had improved so fully she canceled her surgery.

While the Zofran dissolved on my tongue, the acrid flavor of fake bubblegum sweetness promising at least marginal relief of the nausea threatening to make me leave the service, I felt caught in the tension between her story and mine.

With tears streaming down her face, she testified to the church, "God sees you. My breathing issues were small enough that I hadn't even thought to ask God to heal them, but he did. He cares about even the smallest parts of our lives."

Two others followed her, describing stories of radical change.

I marveled at these stories and rejoiced to hear them. It is undeniable that God sometimes heals sickness, removes struggles, and brings new life in stunning ways now, even as we wait for the full expression of his kingdom to come. But sitting in present pain and nausea, in a body God has not chosen to heal, I wondered, *When was the last time I heard a story like mine in church? Would a story of someone being sustained in ongoing suffering rather than having it removed ever be valued enough to be shared from the front of this church?*

I glanced around the sanctuary, taking stock of the stories I knew it held—marriages ending in divorce, jobs lost, empty wombs, terminal brain cancer, chronic Lyme disease. I wondered, *What story are these saints being shaped to expect? And if that story doesn't come true, will they be strong enough to perceive God as kind even if he doesn't remove the small and large struggles in their lives?*

When the church amplifies stories of healing and overcoming without also elevating stories of sustaining grace, she is not adequately forming souls to hold on to hope. If the majority of stories we hear are tales of triumph, we will question the worth of our stories when healing doesn't come. God, in his wisdom, in his hidden purposes, allows some of our suffering to linger, and the church unintentionally turns hearts away from the heart of God when she does not hold space for the sacred mystery that weakness reveals God's strength.

Without understanding that the story of Scripture includes suffering until Jesus returns, we will place unnecessary burdens on ourselves and others to heal or hide pain that persists. The good news of the gospel on this side of Christ's return is that God is redeeming all that is broken *and* is holding all things together while we wait for the fullness of his redemption. The church only offers half her good news when she does not make space to share and honor stories of suffering that lingers.

As Jesus prepared his disciples for his death, he spoke these words: "Truly I tell you, you will weep and mourn, but the world will rejoice. You will become sorrowful, but your sorrow will turn to joy. When a woman is in labor, she has pain because her time has come. But when she has given birth to a child, she no longer remembers the suffering because of the joy that a person has been born into the world. So you also have sorrow now. But I will see you again. Your hearts will rejoice, and no one will take away your joy from you."[3]

Jesus' words to his disciples are just as true for us today. We will weep and mourn. We will have sorrow. And our sorrow will turn to joy. Today, in the tension of pain that persists, we are living the reality Jesus named. Here we find the descending, rising rhythm that creates our new life. As Henri Nouwen says, "It is the way in which pain can be embraced, not out of a desire to suffer, but in the knowledge that something new will be born in the pain."[4] In our longing for tension to be relieved, we cannot miss that Jesus said sorrow comes before joy. This is the church's story: sorrow comes before the song.

The apostle Peter echoed Jesus' words, encouraging believers

....
3 John 16:20–22.
4 Henri J. M. Nouwen, *Here and Now: Living in the Spirit* (New York: Crossroad, 1994), 47.

to stand firm in suffering instead of being surprised by it: "Dear friends, don't be surprised when the fiery ordeal comes among you to test you as if something unusual were happening to you. Instead, rejoice as you share in the sufferings of Christ, so that you may also rejoice with great joy when his glory is revealed."[5]

Peter said we shouldn't be surprised when suffering comes, but I was—and occasionally still am—when sickness and disappointments came crashing with fresh intensity. And you probably were too. You might still be surprised that suffering remains in your story.

Peter's words encourage us not to be surprised but to rejoice, a shift that feels like a wild, almost insane leap in the middle of sobbing. His words make me wonder if rejoicing starts by reminding ourselves to not be surprised. Maybe we experience the joy of our suffering being connected to the suffering of Christ by first choosing to accept its existence in our lives. Maybe joy emerges in the tenacious choice to not be surprised or ashamed of suffering, no matter what our churches or culture seem to shout.

Just a few sentences farther along in this passage, Peter exhorted his readers to be aware of the reality that the devil prowls like a lion looking to attack and devour anyone he can: "Resist him, firm in the faith, knowing that the same kind of sufferings are being experienced by your fellow believers throughout the world."[6]

Part of our resistance to being devoured by suffering is being aware that suffering is the shared experience of the people of God all over the world. When our suffering is hidden behind closed doors and strained smiles, it's difficult to remember the truth. It's hard to remember you aren't the only one afflicted when you can't see anyone else's tears. But the tears are there, waiting to be witnessed. We rise in resistance to the devil's schemes when we remember

....
5 1 Peter 4:12–13.
6 1 Peter 5:9.

we are not the only ones suffering and choose to keep seeing and embracing the poor, pitiable, and oppressed in our midst, including ourselves. Remembering suffering's existence is resistance.

James also writes to the church as though suffering was expected: "Consider it a great joy, my brothers and sisters, *whenever* you experience various trials, because you know that the testing of your faith produces endurance."[7]

James used the word *whenever*, not *if*. Suffering is not just for some of us; it is something every Christian will experience. And it is because suffering is expected and because of the tension it creates that James writes toward the end of his letter, "Therefore, brothers and sisters, be patient until the Lord's coming. . . . Strengthen your hearts, because the Lord's coming is near. . . . Brothers and sisters, take the prophets who spoke in the Lord's name as an example of suffering and patience. See, we count as blessed those who have endured."[8]

These are words to the weary, counsel to those watching closely for Jesus to return. Endurance in suffering is the story of God's people being formed into wholeness. Sitting in the place of our suffering prepares us to sit on thrones in Christ's kingdom,[9] for "blessed is the one who endures trials, because when he has stood the test he will receive the crown of life that God has promised to those who love him."[10]

The apostle Paul also describes suffering as a central, unifying experience of followers of Jesus. He writes that God "comforts us in all our affliction, so that we may be able to comfort those who are in any kind of affliction, through the comfort we ourselves receive from God."[11]

....
7   James 1:2–3, emphasis added.
8   James 5:7, 8, 10–11.
9   Luke 22:30; Rev. 20:4.
10 James 1:12.
11 2 Cor. 1:4.

Paul describes a participation in suffering that assumes it will happen, and his words place suffering in the context of community. To him, suffering was not about private pain but about shared comfort: "If we are afflicted, it is for your comfort and salvation. If we are comforted, it is for your comfort, which produces in you patient endurance of the same sufferings that we suffer."[12]

The church can multiply comfort and amplify endurance through becoming a fellowship where suffering is named as normal. It is not our whole story, but it is part of it. Hope rises when we remind each other of what Jesus told his disciples: "I have told you these things so that in me you may have peace. You *will* have suffering in this world. Be courageous! I have conquered the world."[13]

Christ's ultimate victory over death fills us with confidence that suffering is not the end of our story. Rather it is the sacred space where God's Spirit fills us with courage to express his power and presence in a world where darkness is passing away.

We are a people waiting in expectation for the day when God will make all things new. We are also a people of presence; Christ is in us and in our midst now. Grace is not always rescue. It is often Christ's presence meeting us in weakness and sustaining us in sorrow. Grace is not just power to overcome. It is power to endure.

We who suffer are here to tell the church that the space we hold for suffering in our public gatherings and private conversations directly shapes the maturity of every saint in our midst to hold and experience her Living Hope.

We who weep are here to warn the church that unless we make room to bear witness to weakness, we'll hand out half-hearted hope.

....
12 2 Cor. 1:6.
13 John 16:33, emphasis added.

We who hurt are here to remind the church that the stories worth telling are not just the ones where pain ends but where God sustains. Because when the church doesn't shape saints to expect affliction, she doesn't guide us to encounter our suffering, risen Lord. We aren't well-prepared to offer and receive the ministry of Christ's presence, because we aren't well-prepared to acknowledge suffering that isn't short-term. Remembering the place suffering holds in the story of God empowers us to acknowledge and respect its place in one another's stories rather than cowering in corners or judging from perceived strength.

The space the church offers to recall and express the reality of suffering directly shapes our expectations of the grace we can receive in it. When the main thrust of our liturgies is the triumph of the resurrection, those who strongly sense the dirt of the grave might eventually feel pushed right out the church's back door. Jesus' story included dying, and if we don't regularly sing and speak the reality of lament, we won't see our stories rising in the upward trajectory of his resurrection.

I wonder what our lives would look like if the church intentionally made room for suffering. I'm curious about how much more hope we could hold if worship services included half as much time for lament as they do for praise. I wonder how much encouragement we might all be missing by treating each other's ongoing suffering like an awkward subject to avoid rather than a normal experience to share.

I wonder how much less anguish we would experience in suffering if the church treated suffering like a story to tell rather than a secret to keep until it passes.

Instead of approaching and analyzing ongoing struggles and disappointments as indications of a lack of faith or the absence of God's presence, Jesus reminded his disciples to remember suffering's existence so that we could dwell in his peace. We can't repeat his words enough: "I have told you these things so that *in me you may have peace*. You will have suffering in this world. Be courageous! I have conquered the world."[14]

No matter what our churches or the culture around us says, our Lord said to expect suffering and to expect his peace. When we step courageously into the reality he named, we show the rest of the church and the watching world that God has not forgotten the weak, the poor, the odd, or the needy. When we let suffering be seen as part of our stories, we remind others that suffering is a valuable, sacred part of following Jesus Christ. As we do, the continuing presence of disease, disorders, weakness, trauma, and poverty become stories of Christ's solidarity and places to see his lordship touch everything.

God has not closed his eyes to the pain of his world. And we must not either. I've tried many times to close my eyes to darkness, hoping it would help me see light. I've turned my gaze from my own pain and sin and the hurts of humans both near and far, and I've found the sight that generates the most hope is the one that faces evil squarely, steadily, and compassionately. Open eyes and hearts hold the most grace. I find compelling truth in the words of theologian and philosopher Nicholas Wolterstorff in *Lament for a Son:* "We're in it together, God and we, together in the history of our world. The history of our world is the history of our suffering together. Every evil act extracts a tear from God, every plunge into anguish extracts a sob from God. But also the history of our world is the history of our deliverance together."[15]

The frayed edges of your suffering become lines to trace to joy when you see they aren't borders but threads, tying you to others, tethering you to hope. Your suffering is a woven thread in a tapestry

....
14   John 16:33, emphasis added.
15   Nicholas Wolterstorff, *Lament for a Son* (Grand Rapids: Eerdmans, 1987), 91.

of transformation. Its beauty is most evident not as a singular strand but as one of many intertwined fibers, holding each other's weight, forming a textured picture of being the image of God. When the church sees suffering as a chapter in her story of joy, she can weave together loose, weak threads. She can form a tapestry of wholeness where there was isolation and hidden darkness. She can embody the sight of God.

You are never too sick, too needy, too sad, or too odd for God's kingdom. Church, if Jesus said his power is perfected in weakness, maybe we should spend less energy treating weakness as a problem to fix and more time bearing witness to it with expectation of seeing Christ.

Every church lives and reinforces an embodied story.[16] We have to consider the story we are being shaped by. And we must ask ourselves honestly if we will contribute to the reshaping of our shared story.

We belong to each other, and our life together as a body forms both our hope and the fullness of our participation in God's story of redemption. We are embodied, socially embedded creatures, and as such, we are shaped most deeply not simply by what we hear in sermons but by our physical and social experience of being with and among the body of Christ.[17] Christianity "is not a set of beliefs or doctrines one believes in order to be a Christian, but rather," ethicist and theologian Stanley Hauerwas argues, "Christianity is to have one's body shaped, one's habits determined, in such a way that the worship of God is unavoidable."[18]

....
16 See chapter 9, "The Embodied Church," in Warren S. Brown and Brad D. Strawn, *The Physical Nature of Christian Life: Neuroscience, Psychology, and the Church* (New York: Cambridge Univ. Press, 2012), 140-57.
17 Ibid.
18 Stanley Hauerwas, "The Sanctified Body," in *Embodied Holiness*, ed. Samuel M. Powell and Michael E. Lodahl (Downers Grove, IL: InterVarsity Press, 1999), 22.

The church's gathered presence in worship can both form and fragment our likeness to Christ. Embodied experiences in gathered, corporate worship that capture all five of our senses carry the power of absorbing Christ's memory farther into our own. Because we have embodied, relational minds, when we gather together, our shared presence, postures, and habits are either reinforcing old neural networks or forming and strengthening new pathways of peace, hope, joy, and love. Liturgies shape us in conscious and unconscious ways, moving us toward a specific goal.[19] The question is, how are we shaping each other? Are we moving one another toward a kingdom of consumeristic self-sufficiency or the kingdom of communion?

The church needs the embodied witness of weakness to fully inhabit the true story of God's kingdom. In 1 Corinthians, Paul challenges the church in Corinth to be strengthened in the way of Jesus instead of divided and distracted by rivalries and the wealth, worldly wisdom, and immorality of their culture. He reminds the Corinthians that "Christ is the power of God and the wisdom of God, because God's foolishness is wiser than human wisdom, and God's weakness is stronger than human strength."[20]

In a culture fueled by fear, where the weakest are denigrated by the powerful and cast into dark, dank places, out of sight, while the rest of the country tries to march happily on, we need to listen closely to Paul's subversive, challenging words. God has chosen what is weak in the world to show his wisdom. God has chosen what is small and despised to most show his great love.[21] The parts of the

19 Brad D. Strawn and Warren S. Brown, "Liturgical Animals: What Psychology and Neuroscience Tell Us about Formation and Worship," *Liturgy* 28, no. 4 (2013): 11.

20 1 Cor. 1:24–25.

21 1 Cor. 1:27–28.

body of Christ we most don't want to be or see are the parts Paul says are indispensable.[22]

We who are weak remind the entire church that salvation comes only through God and not through our self-sufficient striving. Our cries help the church hear the truth that our shared story is not finished. The mighty kingdom of God has not fully come, and the small kingdoms of this world offer only a puny, plastic imitation of the freedom and joy we were made for.[23]

We who mourn carry vision the world needs. Through the lenses of tears, we can truly see.[24] Something is broken that God will make whole. We who grieve call the church's attention back to those to whom Jesus directed the majority of his attention— the poor, the widows, the orphans, the marginalized, disabled, doubting, and weak. We remember Christ, Croatian theologian Miroslav Volf writes, "by reenacting his solidarity with the victims of oppression."[25]

We grieve because we have seen flashes of the beauty and joy and pure love of the kingdom of God. And we ache for it to come. The church most displays the heart of God when she is willing to remain in the mystery that it is the tears of the saints mingling with God's that water the tree of life God is growing to heal this world.[26]

The church needs to rediscover the worship of repositioning

....

22 1 Cor. 12:22.

23 Kate Bowler writes, "What would it mean for Christians to give up that little piece of the American Dream that says, 'You are limitless'? Everything is not possible. The mighty kingdom of God is not yet here. What if 'rich' did not have to mean 'wealthy,' and 'whole' did not have to mean 'healed'? What if being the people of 'the gospel' meant that we are simply people with good news? God is here. We are loved. It is enough." Kate C. Bowler, *Everything Happens for a Reason: And Other Lies I've Loved* (New York: Random House, 2018), 21.

24 In his memoir lamenting his wife's dementia, Douglas Groothuis writes, "Seeing through tears may be the truest seeing of all—at least on this side of paradise." Douglas Groothuis, *Walking through Twilight: A Wife's Illness, a Philosopher's Lament* (Downers Grove, IL: InterVarsity Press, 2017), 86.

25 Miroslav Volf, *The End of Memory: Remembering Rightly in a Violent World* (Grand Rapids: Eerdmans, 2006), 114.

26 Rev. 22:2.

the brokenness of humanity. When we suffer, we sometimes lose sight of ourselves, our worth, and who we are beyond our diagnoses, disappointments, struggles, and grief. Maybe we lose ourselves because our communities have let us. Maybe the reason why we lose sight of our worth as indispensable vessels of weakness that show the world God's strength is because our communities continue to treat weakness like an inconvenience or an avoidable, temporary problem.[27] Who in the church is going to give value back to those the Word says are indispensable?

When we treat suffering predominantly as a problem to eradicate or ignore, we throw away all the depth it reveals about the reality of being human in a world God is making new. As Thomas Merton warned, "A society whose whole idea is to eliminate suffering and bring all its members the greatest amount of comfort and pleasure is doomed to be destroyed. It does not understand that all evil is not necessarily to be avoided."[28]

We who can't hide our weakness help every member of the body see their own places of hidden weakness and pain. As we courageously share our stories of suffering and allow others to see our whole selves, we give permission to others to do the same. Bearing witness to weakness helps us *all* place empty hands on the empty cross, forming expectant hearts for the risen Christ who is coming again to heal, restore, and redeem.

The year I stopped working at the Chalmers Center, I arrived at church most Sundays on edge, my body anticipating the discomfort of difference and the frustration of answering yet another "How are

27 My thinking on this has been profoundly shaped by the work of disability theologian John Swinton. John Swinton, *Dementia: Living in the Memories of God* (Grand Rapids: Eerdmans, 2012).

28 Thomas Merton, *No Man Is an Island* (New York: Barnes and Noble, 1983), 83.

you feeling?" with the disappointing answer that I was, yep, still really sick.

I'd shift in the wooden pew—they really aren't made for bodies like mine—and wistfully watch the other twentysomethings lifting their hands in praise. Their effortless stand-and-sit seemed like a dazzling taunt next to my inability to rise with ease. It wasn't a sitting-friendly church, which was part of why I loved it. I loved the clapping, swaying joy of our multicultural worship, the way our church painted a small picture of the redeemed new earth, where every tribe, tongue, and nation will worship the Lamb together in unity. But in a body that couldn't sway without a groan, I felt frustrated.

After church I would often sob or swear. (That year, it seemed my soul mostly knew how to crumble or cuss.) But one particular Sunday, the only tears I left with were good, the only words praise.

Every week, our quirky little church practiced the tradition of forming one large circle to receive communion together. As we crammed too close for comfort against the walls, every face was visible. We'd sing while receiving the bread and wine, handed with words spoken with utmost intention from church leaders who looked you in the eyes.

In such a circle, you cannot hide.

While everyone else stood, I self-consciously sat in a chair squashed between two seemingly-able bodies in a space much smaller and more exposed than I preferred. The songs were just too long for me to make it through standing. I burned inside with the shame of difference, of not being able to do something that seemed so simple. Surrounded by people, I felt alone. And everyone could see me crying.

A man handed me a chunk of bread. "The body of Christ, broken for you."

A broken body, I thought. Broken like mine, sitting in a chair while everyone else stood.

Another man placed a tiny plastic cup of wine in my shaking hands, too inflamed to grasp it from the tray myself. "The blood of Christ, poured out for you."

I looked up to see a friend looking down at me, meeting my shame-filled eyes with a soft glance, a smile of respect. Suddenly I knew: Jesus as broken was Jesus for me. I grasped, seated and broken, that together we held the mystery of faith. Encircled by people I envied and adored, I realized my life is encircled by love. Positioned with open hands in a circle of praise, I realized my suffering is always situated in love.

Communion equalizes and repositions us all.

We all bring our weakness, inadequacy, and memories of harm to the table, receiving with our bodies the truth that only the cross can unite us to love. In the sacrament of communion, we express the embodied truth that we live and move and have our being in Christ as one body. In the Eucharist, the Orthodox theologian Alexander Schmemann reminds us, "we *create the memory of each other,* we identify each other as living *in* Christ and being united with each other in him."[29]

We each come holding hidden pain and longing for full, unending love. In communion our stories are physically situated into the narrative of God's love. His pursuit, solidarity, and imminent return merge with the past and present shattered pieces of our stories, allowing us to remember Jesus with hope larger than any despair.[30]

Communion repositions all of our brokenness into Christ's body and forms us for the day when our bodies will be made new.

To be faithful to God's story of redemption, the church's public

....
29 Alexander Schmemann, *The Eucharist: Sacrament of the Kingdom,* trans. Paul Kachur (Crestwood, NY: St. Vladimir's Seminary Press, 1988), 130.
30 Volf, *The End of Memory,* 115.

witness must be true to the time and place she occupies in the story. We are a people with the presence of Christ in our midst and a people waiting for the wholeness he'll bring. It is only as we stand open-eyed and openhearted together on the taut line of redemption's story that we'll each experience the wonder of sharing in Christ's life. We *all* need our brokenness repositioned under the communion of the cross.

Together at the table, we name the wrong of suffering that Jesus willingly accepted, we name the darkness remaining in our lives, and we remember God has forever crossed the chasm to us with his love. Communion names us rightly—sinners saved by grace, loved children heading toward a greater feast that will satisfy us forever. Together, in our broken bodies holding Christ's broken body, sipping the spilt wine of his obedience, we position our whole selves to yearn for the marriage supper to come.[31] Sometimes we might even taste it.

In church, in pain, my heart gets turned inside out by encountering my aloneness alongside the love that willingly assumed it. My questions lift my hands, from fists to open fingers, ready to receive a body broken. The only answer to the questions hiding in my heart, the ones that hide in your heart too, is an experience. The answer is a reality we receive together in fragile hands.

This faith we possess is not a list of beliefs that remains effectual only when we can feel their truth. The hope we hold is not a bludgeon goading us into submission to a God who punishes.[32] No matter how imperfectly the church holds space for weakness, hope

....
31 Revelation 19.
32 Though Scripture makes it clear that God *does* punish at times, it is important to consider our suffering against the backdrop of Christ's willing absorption of God's rightful, just punishment for all of humanity's sin. He *already* bore the punishment for sin in his body on the cross.

is in her midst. No matter how awkwardly the church encounters our suffering, Jesus Christ is present when we gather. No matter how angry or hopeless I might feel on any given Sunday, the Spirit is there, turning my groans and even eye-rolls into prayers. In Jesus and his church, I discover God has everything to do with my pain. The doubt, the aloneness, the discomfort, and even the agony of a life torn apart by suffering become the canvas to display the stunning work of God uniting us to himself.

When we gather, we encounter the King who chose to suffer so we could live in his love. This faith we possess is participation in a shared reality that touches and transforms the reality of brokenness in our lives. The Spirit takes the substance of a life spread thin by suffering and makes it a canvas on which the colors of God's embodied love turn from dull red to vibrant crimson through encountering the Son of God stricken. When we who suffer show up in church, we allow the Spirit to paint us all into the likeness and story of Christ.

For the body of Christ to faithfully express the love of Christ, she must be willing to dwell in the mystery of her time and place in the story. We must be willing to plant our feet on the tightrope tension between Christ's coming and his return. We must seek and express God's kingdom of healing and restoration while honoring the mystery hidden in the heart of God, of all the ways his kingdom has not yet come in our lives. With fierce faith and humble holiness, the church must be unwilling to wander from the tension of embodying the presence of our redeeming Christ while weeping remains.

So may we be people of hope, willing to be formed by enduring affliction and willing to radically let the rest of the church see our scars long enough to remember our true, shared story. We will have suffering in this world, and as we courageously endure it, the whole church will better know the sustaining power and presence of Christ.

CHAPTER 10

REPENTANCE

All of Life Is an Opportunity for Communion

> The core message of the gospel is that God invades us
> with new life, but the setting for this most often is the
> ordinariness of our lives. The new life takes place in
> the place and person of our present. It is not a means
> by which God solves problems. God creates new life.
> He is not a problem solver but a person creator.
>
> —EUGENE PETERSON, *AS KINGFISHERS CATCH FIRE*

We want a gospel that tells us we are beloved and safe, but we don't like remembering it also includes death.[1] We want to be protagonists in the story of love, but we need continual conversion to inhabit the place Christ bought for us in his story. The grasp of decay is too tight on our old selves for freedom to be our automatic, constant reality, unless we respond to a different reality, unless we continually turn toward the existence of grace and the

---

1 Theologian William Willimon, reflecting on Jesus' baptism, writes, "Whatever the gospel means, we tell ourselves, it could not mean death." William Willimon, "Repent," in *Bread and Wine: Readings for Lent and Easter* (Maryknoll, NY: Orbis, 2014), 7.

pace of its unhurried, never-ending pursuit.[2] The only way we will break the vise grip of sin and the frantic stride of fear and shame is, as theologian William Willimon asserts, "to be transferred to another dominion, to be cut loose from our old certainties, to be thrust under the flood and then pulled forth fresh and newborn. Baptism takes us there."[3]

Jesus started his public ministry standing on the muddy banks of the Jordan River with a striking act of submission one might assume he didn't need. Jews from all over Judea and Jerusalem were coming to John to be baptized and to confess their sins as a sign of repentance because the kingdom of heaven had come near.[4] Then Jesus came from Galilee and asked John to thrust him under the same dirty water to respond to the reality he had come to inaugurate. The man whose breath formed every atom of hydrogen and oxygen yielded to the symbol and submersion of water. Plunging backward by John's hands into the river's saline coolness, Jesus turned his whole body and whole self toward God in a posture of willing relinquishment, aligning himself and his coming ministry with the will of his Father that would lead him to the cross and to death. And as the water rushed past his rising body, "the heavens suddenly opened for him, and he saw the Spirit of God descending like a dove and coming down on him. And a voice from heaven said: 'This is my beloved Son, with whom I am well-pleased.'"[5]

The Father spoke across time and space to acknowledge

....

2   J. R. R. Tolkien writes, "As the hound follows the hare, never ceasing in its running, ever drawing nearer in the chase, with unhurrying and steady pace, so does God follow the fleeing soul by his divine grace. And though in sin or in human love, away from God it seeks to hide itself, divine grace follows after, unwearyingly follows ever after, till the soul feels its pressure forcing it to turn to him alone in that never ending pursuit." J. R. R. Tolkien, taken from *The Neumann Press Book of Verse* (Long Prairie, MN: Neumann Press, 1988), quoted in James Davison Hunter, *To Change the World: The Irony, Tragedy, and Possibility of Christianity Today* (New York: Oxford Univ. Press, 2010), 242.

3   Willimon, "Repent," 9–10.

4   Matt. 3:2.

5   Matt. 3:16–17.

Jesus both as his Son and as willingly obedient to the waters that foreshadowed his death.[6] Hearing his voice across centuries and cultures today, we catch the tonic of their relationship, the central sound upon which all the music of God's love revolves and extends. It is communion, sonship, a loving trust formed and expressed in both the massive and the mundane.[7] It is the sound and reality we are constantly offered as adopted daughters and sons of God, united to Jesus by faith and being renewed by his Spirit day by day. "When we are baptized," Julie Canlis affirms, "we pass through the waters (which signify death) into *this relationship*—and into this declaration of divine love, spoken for us as well."[8]

On the banks of the Jordan River, turning toward his Father with trust, Jesus heard the words we cannot hear on our own: "You are my beloved." Standing in the mud of our ordinary lives, Jesus still hears what we strain to believe and trains us to hear *beloved* in every mundane and even miserable moment we encounter.[9]

Jesus let the Father's voice of love saturate his entire being. His every thought and action proceeded from the deep inner knowledge that he was wholly, irrevocably loved by God.[10] The sound of his Father's delight sustained him as he faced temptation, isolation, mocking, pain, and even death. And Jesus receives the Father's words of love with joy on our behalf today, the words that sometimes sound cruelly untrue when suffering descends like a dark cloud over our lives.

....

6   Julie Canlis, *A Theology of the Ordinary* (Wenatchee, WA: Godspeed, 2017), 34–35.

7   My thinking about communion has been profoundly influenced by the writing of theologian John Zizioulas, whose work describes the heart of being human as reflecting the life of the Trinity in communion with God and one another. John Zizioulas, *Being as Communion: Studies in Personhood and the Church* (Crestwood, NY: St. Vladimir's Seminary Press, 1997) and *Communion and Otherness: Further Studies in Personhood and the Church* (New York: T&T Clark, 2006).

8   Canlis, *A Theology of the Ordinary,* 34.

9   Ibid., 35.

10   Henri J. M. Nouwen, *Reaching Out,* special ed. (Grand Rapids: Zondervan, 1998), 159.

My husband and I are still picking up the pieces of our shattered life after abrupt and painful job transitions. We don't know where we'll live beyond next month or how we'll pay for my health insurance when our meager savings run out in four months. I've also been battling a sinus infection for weeks, exhausted from pressure and pain. I could easily interpret the misery and mishaps of recent events as a negation of God's love. Can I hear I am beloved by God *here?* Can you learn to hear you are loved in the middle of your hardest, darkest, most exhausting nights?

Our old self has clogged ears and cloudy vision, and in the darkness, we try to create the sound of belovedness on our own through both striving and self-rejection. We block God's words of love in our ordinary lives through an incessant, unaware belief that God wouldn't, couldn't, be loving us in this and that we must make up for his absence in workaholism, image-maintenance, and a constant fear that guards ourselves against failure. We reject our own lives by not giving our weakness attention, our bodies care, and our relationships room to breathe and root.

Relationships are often the places where we've incurred the most pain in life, and they are also the mysterious means God will use to reshape us to live in the story more lasting than pain. Some of us are in the process of being healed and restored from a lifetime of people wounding us. Not being heard, seen, and loved when we needed to be often leads to living hurt, ashamed, and isolated. Without meaning or wanting to, we perpetuate that storyline in the ways we relate with walls up and expectations of ourselves and others that are both too low and too high. Grace asks us to become aware of our tendency to resist love, stay stuck in self-pity, and treat others as both our saviors and ticking time bombs that will hurt us soon.

Our old self stops our ears from hearing God's voice of love in suffering, but in Christ we have been given a new self with new ears and eyes, which is being renewed in knowledge according to the image of Jesus.[11] Our old self, with its plugged ears and poor vision, must be plunged under the cold, cleansing water of the baptism of repentance.

Baptism signifies repentance, which biblically has its root in the Greek word *metanoia,* meaning a "change of mind" that involves turning from sin and turning toward God.[12] In the baptism of Jesus and our own, we find the drowning of our old way of being and the rising of our new selves, turned toward God and aligned with his heart of love. We find a steady invitation from God to commune with him as his beloved children in the current situations and relationships in our lives. We glimpse the gaze of God toward Jesus and hear the blessing he bestows as ours when we reposition ourselves to be present in our ordinary, suffering-filled lives with an expectation to hear, *You are loved.*

"God crosses the universe and comes to us," writes Simone Weil.[13] We think he's far, but God has already come near in Christ and is always present, asking for our attention in our bodies, our circumstances, the beauty of his world, and our yearning for its renewal. The uniqueness of suffering is the continual grief it brings that can prompt us to turn toward the God who is already near. Godly grief really can produce repentance.[14]

To be transformed by the renewing of our minds,[15] we need to present our bodies, as they are now, in the circumstances they are in now, to God as places for worship and communion. We need to

....

11 Col. 3:10.
12 William W. Vine, *The New Strong's Concise Concordance and Vine's Concise Dictionary* (Nashville: Nelson, 1999), 311.
13 Simone Weil, "The Love of God and Affliction," in *Simone Weil: Essential Writings,* ed. Eric O. Springsted (Maryknoll, NY: Orbis, 1998), 53.
14 2 Cor. 7:10.
15 Rom. 12:1-2.

turn from the patterns of our old self that lead to disconnection from others and disintegration within our minds and turn toward God, others, and ourselves with expectancy that grace is here.

In the exhaustion of pain, heartbreak, and ongoing weakness, turning can feel like the last breath that might kill us. We question how we can hope for connection when connection or its absence has left us wounded. How can we worship when we are being pummeled? Christ in us, Christ before us, Christ beside us.[16] His faith, his trust, and his obedience in the hard places of his own humanity fuel us with grace to be faithful in ours. His belief in being God's beloved is the grace the Spirit suffuses into our weary bodies as we turn to acknowledge that God is with us in every place, person, and moment we encounter. Turning is relinquishing the old self, letting our lust for comfort, protection, and prestige fall like dirty rags next to the water of our rebirth, and then inhabiting our new self by engaging with sight, smell, hearing, touch, and taste the reality that God is personally present now. The shape of resurrection is formed in us as we treat our ordinary lives as worth experiencing.

How do we learn to hear *beloved* even and especially in our places of suffering? We repent.

Repentance. It's a word that might make you instantly feel angry or transported back in time to a stuffy Sunday school classroom with flannel board depictions of Bible stories and little grace for being the stubborn, impetuous, or wildly curious child you secretly were inside. (Okay, maybe that was just me.) Repentance makes me think of sin, which reminds me of judgment, which makes me feel shame. And if you are like me, you might be starting to wonder if this book is going to end with you bleeding into a pool of guilt on top of the discouragement you already feel from prolonged suffering.

....

16 Saint Patrick's prayer is cited in Marilyn Chandler McEntyre, *Christ, My Companion: Meditations on the Prayer of St. Patrick* (Eugene, OR: Wipf and Stock, 2008), 10.

What if everything we assume about repentance creates a sense of guilt and shame because we forget to put repentance in the context of communion with God and the great grace that invites, seeks, and restores us to love?

What if there is more room for meaning and joy in our suffering when our lives are empowered by grace to turn and be present here and now in the mundane, repetitive parts of our lives we wish we could escape?

What if repentance is the grace of God, attracting us to life, pulling us into a story where the weak and small matter, and turning us loose to extend life in every corner of creation that has been darkened by the curse of shame?

What if I told you that instead of bleeding out with greater guilt than you already have, you could experience repentance as the continuous repositioning that transfuses you with the powerful, redeeming blood of Christ that will sustain you in your suffering and transform you into a person who believes they are loved?

Repentance is turning, again and again, toward God, others, and our lives with our whole bodies, whole stories, and whole selves to live in the better story that we are united to the God who is present and who redeems. *Repentance is remembering that all of life is an opportunity for communion and choosing to live as such right now.*

Suffering and trauma have the power to scribble *forsaken, forgotten,* and *worthless* all over our hearts and brains, marking our memory and tuning its guidance of our everyday experiences into the overwhelming sound of shame. To hear the voice of love and to let our lives, stories, and brains be reshaped and rewritten by God's presence, we have to pay attention. If we are not captivated by the story and presence of grace, we'll live captive to the story of shame. Attention is the activity of repentance. It is "imagination put in the harness of faith,"[17] the eager expectation that God is as present as he says he is and will do what he says he will do.

We need more than preaching to ourselves to dwell in the truth that we are loved. Truth is more than a bandaid we place repeatedly over our fear with reminders of what is right. Truth is a Presence to absorb in embodied experiences that employ all five of our senses with the indelible ink that renames us loved and good. The graffiti defacing our neural pathways with the message that we aren't really loved and aren't really safe is scoured in the repentance of experiencing our everyday lives with attention, intention, and imagination. Directing our attention, Dan Siegel explains, has "the power to shape our brain's firing patterns, as well as the power to shape the architecture of the brain itself."[18] Attention is the fertilizer that strengthens and nourishes our abiding in the Vine of Jesus and his body.

If I want to hear God's voice calling me loved in the middle of circumstances I can't wish away, I paradoxically have to direct my attention to experience my circumstances more fully. My brain, body, and story will be changed not in simply pining after relief but in being present in my ordinary, often hard life because Scripture tells me my body and life are places God has chosen to indwell and redeem. Instead of trying to shield myself from all the bad things I seem to attract like fruit draws flies, I can shift from mindlessly detaching from my life to mindfully witnessing and encountering it as a place full of grace, meaning, and potential for goodness. Attention is faith embodied, the power the Spirit uses to retune our whole selves to the rhythm of grace inviting us to dwell in love.

Will we turn—again and again—toward the place where we are named as loved and toward the God who speaks our name?[19]

....

17 Eugene H. Peterson, *A Long Obedience in the Same Direction: Discipleship in an Instant Society* (Downers Grove, IL: InterVarsity Press, 2000), 144.

18 Daniel J. Siegel, *Mindsight: The New Science of Personal Transformation* (New York: Bantam, 2011), 39.

19 Thomas Merton writes, "We get a name in baptism. That is because the depths of our soul are stamped, by that holy sacrament, with a supernatural identification

_⚓_

I come to the water like a baptism, to submerge myself in a better story and to rise again, dripping, with a stronger song. The red bird of paradise flowers on my swimsuit are stiff and crinkly from my swim two days ago, but my spirit is flooded, my body awash with fear, anger, and a sprinkling of self-contempt.

Ryan just reworked our budget, and I nearly had a panic attack considering how long it will take us to pay off debt we've accrued trying to treat and survive my illness. For all the frequency with which I preach the gospel that weakness is a place to know God's strength, I'm still ashamed that in our weakness, we haven't been able to maintain the standard of fiscal responsibility we inherited from our parents. We were prepared for a life of capably providing for ourselves, but no one prepared us for the poverty of my broken body. No one prepared us for a decade of deciding between getting treatment and buying groceries, knowing that choosing one means not being able to afford the other.

White Protestant culture's story that frugality married with effort produces success is a narrative we've tried and failed to fulfill. We look the part—educated, hardworking, churchgoing, and cloaked with pearlescent skin—but each MRI costs five hundred dollars, and each monthly infusion of immunotherapy retails at ten thousand dollars. Last year I counted the days I was sick with infections on top of my normal level of illness: five whole months out of twelve. Sometimes I wonder if money is the material in our lives most untouched by the gospel. In our bank accounts and leather wallets, we hide the last vestiges of individualism's gospel that we each can secure a life with minimal pain on our own.

....

which will eternally tell us who we were meant to be. Our baptism, which drowns us in the death of Christ, summons upon us all the sufferings of our life: their mission is to help us work out the pattern of our identity received in the sacrament." Thomas Merton, *No Man Is an Island* (New York: Barnes and Noble, 2003), 81.

Even though I'm too sick to be a character in the success story, I'm drenched by its shame.

One thing my culture's story got right is that effort does matter. What makes the difference is whom our effort is in response to. Are we reacting to our own cavernous emptiness or responding to a fullness sensed behind our bones and beyond our yearning? Am I trying to build my own blessings? Or am I answering a grace that stoops to places lower than I want to dwell, a God who crosses the universe to speak life in the silence of both beauty and affliction?[20]

I know that without attention, I'll keep living flooded by the shame of a story that's not true.

I come to the water to be baptized in a better story. With each barefoot step onto coarse concrete, I'm seeking a different kind of effort, the agency of attention given to a story where those who are weak are named loved. Plunging into chlorinated coolness, I start the slow trek of inhabiting my anxious body in the water's enveloping grace.

Elongating from torso to toes, my spine straight, I let the rhythm of the burden that brought me to the pool slow in the cadence of strokes and breath. My arms slice through blue water, and what was stressed becomes strong. With each gulp, I take in more than oxygen.

This body

is loved

by God.

The what-ifs and whys of our past, present, and future gradually hush alongside the inaudible wake of my deliberate breathing.

Each inhalation an acknowledgment.

This body

Every exhalation a resolve.

----

20 Simone Weil asserts that there are two things piercing enough to penetrate our souls with the love of God—beauty and affliction. Weil, "The Love of God and Affliction," 41–71.

is loved

Entire breath an attestation.

by God.

Lungs, mind, and heart fill in unison as slow motion matches patient breaths, carrying my whole body and whole self into the ancient story that's always crossing mine. Where I strained, I now savor. The coolness between my toes, the tingling of muscles lengthening, the reverence of remembering: *This body*—the one that disqualifies me from prevailing standards of success—*is loved by God.* Six words, repeated, breathed, and absorbed, re-member me as a person sought, surrounded, and upheld by grace.

When I started swimming again this winter, a quarter of my mental attention was spent trying to not think about the lifeguards judging my clumsy form and the soft shape of my overweight body. Today I'm setting my mind elsewhere, recalling the concept of mental models—how our brains create parcels of patterns of neural firing in response to our environment.[21] Instead of judging my body, I'm pondering how every space we enter prompts a particular parcel to wake up in our minds, which guides our response to that place, what it means and represents to us, and how we are supposed to feel while there. It's why entering a grocery store can mean feeling overwhelmed or why going to work might mean feeling lonely. It's why being at the gym in the pool means I'm wading through shame as well as water.

The brain's innate neuroplasticity, its ability to form new connections and patterns through intention, repetition, and relational attunement, reminds me that how I encounter a place offers possibility to positively change while there.[22] With kindness, attention, and imagination, places that previously evoked shame can

....

21 Curt Thompson, "Create Compassionate Spaces," interview with Jessica Honegger, *Going Scared*, podcast audio, September 12, 2018, *https://jessicahonegger.com/podcast/episode-30-create-compassionate-spaces-with-curt-thompson/*.

22 Siegel, *Mindsight*.

begin to elicit safety, hope, and joy. Taking a sip from my water bottle at the pool's edge, I set out to swim the next five laps, creating a new memory of this place and my effort in it as good and strong.

As I push off the pool's edge, I spring into my own story, to memories of water and myself in it as resilient. While my arms and legs propel me forward, my mind traces time backward to a summer spent as a lifeguard on a reservation in North Carolina. The stamina formed almost fifteen years ago through long laps and youthful pluck stirs new hope in me now. My body remembers being strong and courageous. I follow the map of my memory farther, to girlhood summers spent dancing in shallow water, toes touching cerulean vinyl and arms lifted in pirouettes of praise. Now I paint both the water and my mind with words, joining past and present in a rising resilience that proclaims this body is loved by God.

I came to the water like a baptism, to be drenched in the story deeper than my fear and shame, consenting to be changed. Movement is prayer, memory a font, attention a sacrament. Thirty minutes later I step out of the pool into a shaft of late afternoon light, more wholly believing the words Jesus heard at his own baptism as true and as mine: *You are my beloved; with you I am well-pleased.* Drying off with a warm towel, I make a promise to myself to come back this Thursday if I am at all able.

As the apostle Paul writes, we don't give up. "Even though our outer person is being destroyed, our inner person is being renewed day by day."[23] Because the Spirit that raised Jesus from the dead lives in me, I will never give up on experiencing my life as a place bursting with the grace that turns death into life. New life is possible and immanent in our affliction because God created us to share in the

23 2 Cor. 4:16.

redemptive suffering and resurrection of his Son through communion with Christ and his body. When we don't give up on our lives as places to find grace, God resurrects the flow of energy in our minds to experience him as near and good and ourselves as loved. This is repentance.

The potential for resurrection is woven into the fabric of our being. Neuroscience has been revealing that our brains retain the ability to grow new neurons throughout adulthood, a process called neurogenesis. In 2017 neuroscientists at the University of Alabama at Birmingham found that as adult-born neurons connect to existing neural networks, older neurons die off.[24] And in 2019 neuropathology researchers in Spain found that the hippocampus, the part of the brain most operative in our memory, has the potential for abundant neurogenesis throughout the life span.[25] Our brains are wired to take the path of least resistance, the most energy-efficient way of responding to the world around us, but to change and grow, we have to do what does not come naturally.[26] Repentance, forming our minds into the shape of resurrection, requires doing what does not come naturally. Neurogenesis and, really, new life in Christ require shifting from our automatic, mindless way of reacting to life to an intentional posture of mindfulness and receptivity. Our minds are renewed with the brain's ability to rewire (neuroplasticity) by directing the focus of our attention.[27] Our old memories,

....

24 Elena W. Adlaf et al., "Adult-Born Neurons Modify Excitatory Synaptic Transmission to Existing Neurons," *Elife* (January 30, 2017), *https://elifesciences.org/articles/19886*.

25 Elena P. Moreno-Jiménez et al., "Adult Hippocampal Neurogenesis Is Abundant in Neurologically Healthy Subjects and Drops Sharply in Patients with Alzheimer's Disease," *Nature Medicine* 25 (April 2019): 554–81.

26 Boris Cheval et al., "Avoiding Sedentary Behaviors Requires More Cortical Resources Than Avoiding Physical Activity: An EEG Study," *Neuropsychologia* 119 (October 2018): 68–80.

27 Curt Thompson, "Spirituality, Neuroplasticity, and Personal Growth," interview, Biola University Center for Christian Thought, *The Table*, video, March 7, 2013, *https://cct.biola.edu/spirituality-neuroplasticity-and-personal-growth-curt-thompson-full-interview/*.

along with the neural networks that have been shaped by shame, are transformed as we engage life with intention, as we learn to pay attention to what we are paying attention to, and as we place ourselves in embodied experiences of grace, vulnerability, and connection. The old passes away as new neurons and neural networks are formed in our continual turning toward the space between God, others, and ourselves as the ground where grace is born.

God forms the rising resilience of our new self as we take our everyday, suffering-filled lives and present them to him as places where stress can be soothed in the context of new love and connection. We learn to hear *beloved* in our suffering when we turn to the unhurried rhythm of grace pulsing through both solitude and community.

The practice of spiritual disciplines places our hands on the reality of the kingdom, allowing our time and space to be intersected by God's reign and presence. The classic spiritual disciplines practiced by Christians throughout the ages offer us embodied habits that reshape us as whole people created for love, capable of love, and secure in love. Describing the wealth of practices available to grow our awareness and our abiding in God's love is far beyond the scope of this small book, but Richard Foster's *Celebration of Discipline* is a wonderful place to start familiarizing yourself with practices Christians have used for centuries to dwell as beloved.[28]

Spiritual disciplines form the habit of repentance. The practice of disciplines like contemplative prayer (such as the breath prayer I did while swimming) teaches us to focus our attention, tolerate the present moment, and treat ourselves and others with less judgment.[29] As we turn toward God through spiritual disciplines that

....

28 Richard J. Foster, *Celebration of Discipline: The Path to Spiritual Growth* (New York: HarperOne, 2018).
29 Joshua J. Knabb and Veola E. Vazquez, "A Randomized Controlled Trial of a 2-Week Internet-Based Contemplative Prayer Program for Christians with Daily Stress," *Spirituality in Clinical Practice* 5, no. 1 (March 2018): 37.

expand our capacity for calm in the midst of stress, we grow in our capacity to activate our brain's social engagement system to seek safety and solidarity where we used to automatically shut down.[30] Slowing down paradoxically builds our capacity to persevere and connect.

Repentance is a hospitality of heart to God's heart, holding every moment, molecule, and human connection in an unfolding story that ends not in disappointment but in joy. Grace invites us to change by stepping into that story through trust formed one courageous encounter at a time. Courage is the virtue that empowers repentance.[31] It is choosing to inhabit our broken bodies and imperfect relationships with trust and attention, especially when we are scared, because we believe—even just a tiny bit—that God goes with us and has named us *loved*.

Jesus' command to be courageous in the presence of suffering[32] is one we all can repeatedly attempt to obey with hope because courage is not a possession but a practice. Courage is not the absence of anxiety but the practice of trusting we are held and loved no matter what. It is facing the present moment with open eyes and willingness to participate in God's story of making all things new, even when our world is falling apart, our bodies are breaking in terrible ways, and we don't know how we'll survive one more hard thing.

Repentance forms the shape of the cross and resurrection in our stories as we choose to practice the virtue of courage every

....
30 Jeffrey Zimmerman, "Neuro-Narrative Therapy: Brain Science, Narrative Therapy, Poststructuralism, and Preferred Identities," *Journal of Systemic Therapies* 36, no. 2 (2017): 12–26.
31 As C. S. Lewis writes, "Courage is not simply *one* of the virtues, but the form of every virtue at the testing point, which means, at the point of highest reality." C. S. Lewis, *The Screwtape Letters* (New York: HarperCollins, 2001), 161.
32 John 16:33.

single day. As a virtue, courage forms Christ's life in us over time, as that which is presently difficult slowly becomes the habit of our heart. N. T. Wright elucidates this power: "Virtue . . . is what happens when someone has made a thousand small choices requiring effort and concentration to do something which is good and right, but which doesn't 'come naturally'—and then, on the thousand and first time, when it really matters, they find that they do what's required 'automatically' . . . *virtue* is what happens when wise and courageous choices have become 'second nature.'"[33]

Every moment, every day, we are invited to participate in Love's intersection with time. Repentance is remembering the ever-present possibility of participating in the ever-present kingdom of God. Courage faces the present as a place to participate in Love touching and transforming time. It moves from defeat to desire, accepting and doing the next thing, however small it might be, in faith that we are participating in God's unshakable, lasting kingdom.[34]

Courage is the act of repentance, choosing communion with God and others in the places we feel ashamed, apathetic, rejected, exhausted, distracted, and defeated. It is living our baptismal identity in the daily drowning of our old self and the rising of the new. This morning it was standing under nearly scalding water to soothe my stiff spine, acting in hope that today could hold more than pain. This afternoon it was sensing doubt creeping inside that my writing doesn't matter and others don't care, then stopping work

....
33 N. T. Wright, *After You Believe: Why Christian Character Matters* (New York: HarperCollins, 2010), 20–21.
34 Emily P. Freeman beautifully uses the phrase "do the next right thing in love" in her helpful book *The Next Right Thing: A Simple, Soulful Practice for Making Life Decisions* (Grand Rapids: Revell, 2019). The idea of simply doing the next thing has grounded my life in everyday courage ever since I came across the poem "Do the Next Thing" as a college freshman. In a season of loss and disorientation, I was emboldened by the simplicity not of knowing how I would make it through *everything* but of focusing on just doing and surviving the *next thing*. We can't have faith for all our future days; we have faith for today. Courage to do the next right thing pulls our lives forward in the trajectory of the kingdom and shapes us to be people deeply connected to Jesus because we rely on him for our every step.

to sit still for ten minutes, practicing centering prayer, absorbing the reality that God always cares. Courage is noticing the swell of self-importance and drowning it by considering others' needs. It is refusing to use pain and suffering as an excuse to be irritable and selfish and asking for forgiveness every time I'm mean or dismissive. It is holding a cup of tea across from someone new, holding space in my heart to treat their story as sacred and our connection as possible. Repentance wraps my hands, our hands, around the cross and allows God to form its shape in our lives.

Courage is the virtue the entire body of Christ needs to walk the tightrope tension of God's kingdom coming to recreate this world. Through courage, we respond to God's love by showing up, again and again, to be seen, known, and loved together. Courage empowers us to listen where we normally would defend, to witness pain instead of judging it, to acknowledge failure as room to grow, and to sit with discomfort like it's a dawn, not a death.

Through the virtue of courage, our ordinary lives are transfigured from death to life. Our lives are physiologically and spiritually expanded to see and hear more goodness than our old eyes and ears could perceive. We who have so thoroughly tasted the bitterness of death grow more able to savor the goodness of life. When we stop rejecting our lives by spending all our energy on seeking rescue, we have energy left to taste and see the goodness that is here. We find God's love in the small crevices of a life slowed and shattered by suffering. I sense God's sustaining grace in the scent of the rosemary I just passed, noticing its bloom for the first time and breathing a sigh of relief after working hard all day. I feel the warmth of the evening air on my face and prize its presence in anticipation of tomorrow's chilly rain. I can hold each moment—the beautiful and the brutal—and squeeze it like an orange for all its juice. Here, with Christ in me, with Christ around me, in the presence of friends and family near and far, is there any moment that does not hold the possibility of holy joy? Broken apart by suffering, I now hold space to soak in all of life as places where God is seeking me with joy. We, the fellowship of the broken, become the best holders of joy.

When we live in the courage of repentance, we notice with hope and wonder that God sustains every blossom and breath. And in the noticing, we are sustained and renewed. Joy is a matter of attention, a mediation of being willing to see suffering, an expectancy of gratitude, a hospitality of the heart formed moment by moment as we live our ordinary lives in the presence of the God who is here.

This is your one life. The scorched earth of your suffering—the daily fight of disease, disorders, grief, trauma, abuse, loss, and unrealized dreams and desires—is the ground where God is breathing new life. You won't see it, you won't feel it, you won't become it until you stand on the ground of your life with courage *today*. And when you do, Jesus will stand with you, sustaining you with grace and making you new.

Through repentance, you and I continually turn and discover we are not slaves of suffering or prisoners of pain but daughters and sons, being formed to reign with Jesus over a kingdom that will last.

ACKNOWLEDGMENTS

*We are more aspen than oak, reaching skyward in hope,
glorious in waving gold, both our beauty and survival
formed and sustained in interdependence.*

The truest truth about myself is that I am one whom God loves, and in his love, I am the recipient of the lavish grace of being loved by his people. I am more aspen than oak because of the body of Christ. This book exists because great grace has upheld and nourished me in the form of people scattered across the years of my life, standing with the outstretched hands of Jesus, pulling me into the embrace of redemption. For these words made flesh, I give God thanks.

Mom and Dad, you raised me to be courageous. You steeped my life in the Word of God so thoroughly that when the time came that I couldn't even open the Word, it was still reverberating and audible, hidden in my heart. My tenacity is in large part the inheritance of your example of diligence and grit. McKenzie, my sister, it is a bittersweet honor to learn the courage of repentance alongside you in the crucible of autoimmune disease. Courage is choosing to step into the dark, especially when it is scary, because we know God goes with us. Tenacity is the confidence of courage practiced over time. It is a joy to watch God making you tenacious. Tucker and Marco, my brothers, it has been beautiful to watch you build your families on the foundation of courage these last few years.

Mom and Dad Ramsey, your kindness is a bright spot in my life. Thank you for raising Ryan into the most loyal, kind man I've ever known.

The church has encircled my life in loving-kindness, and though each passing year of my life has further revealed her need for wholeness, I am who I am because of a lifetime planted, rooted, and growing in the local church. To the church of my baptism and childhood and to my pastor, Jim Mascow, thank you for shaping me in the rhythms of grace. PJ, thank you for modeling the heart of Jesus in ordinary, steady faithfulness. To the churches of my adulthood, especially New City East Lake and New City Fellowship, thank you for giving me the sweetest, most tangible taste of the coming kingdom of God I have ever received. Thank you for giving me a vision of God's commitment to the weakest and poorest and for showing the world a small picture of how he is uniting *all* people to one another and himself. To our pastor, Jim Pickett, thank you for leading us in the courage of vulnerability. Your willingness to walk into the dark has made Ryan and me people of light.

This book is the gift of my education, the fruit of many humble, faithful educators who took a nerdy kid who loved learning and taught her that knowledge rooted in love can change the world. I thank God especially for the beauty I encountered at Covenant College in professors and fellow students set aflame in amazement at Christ's love redeeming everything. Kelly Kapic, you shaped me more than you probably realize. From the first day of Doctrine I, your sense of wonder over the majestic mystery of God invited me to live my whole life as worship. Thank you for seeing potential in my words, connecting me to Zondervan, and offering encouragement along the way.

The message of this book is that grace is found in the body of Christ, and I figured if I was going to write that, then I had better live it, down to the dirt of how this book was crafted. These words were formed and upheld by a literary community, for whom I am especially grateful because this book happened to be written during one of the hardest set of circumstances I have ever endured. Thank you to my writing friends for pouring encouragement into me through every step of this process. You each embody the wisdom of the kingdom, that scarcity is a lie and abundance is both our inheritance and our surprising method. We raise our voices in a chorus that is stronger and sweeter because it is shared. Meredith McDaniel, your kindness has been like manna in a desert. Lore Wilbert, your friendship has helped me relearn how to trust, and your support of my words has helped me better believe who I am in Christ. Bethany Rydmark, your tireless willingness to share life with me across a million Voxer messages has been such a surprising, fun gift. I can't thank you enough for gathering Team K.J. to pray me through those grueling, final weeks of finishing my manuscript. Team K.J., when I think of how you prayed, sent messages, cards, gifts, and even my favorite flowers (peonies!), my eyes well up with tears. Summer Gross, Jodi Grubbs, Valerie Murray, Jena Meyerpeter, Heather Legge, Sue Fulmore, Jenna Dunson, Julianna Chapman, Susan Ely, Katie Casselberry, Carol Collier, and Heidi Saballos, your generosity to pray really did spiritually lift my arms to keep typing when I was at the end of my strength. (Faith really is a communal fire we stoke together.) Thelma Nienhuis, thank you for being the giddiest supporter of my book. Your kindness is beautiful. Ronne Rock, sharing deadlines and prayers with you has been a gift. Chuck DeGroat, thank you for speaking with clarity and tenderness into my writing and trauma and for reading early bits of this book. To my larger writing community through hope*writers, thank you for being a community where generosity is the norm. Thank you to my agent, Andrew Wolgemuth. Your kindness and wisdom have infused me with strength in times when I felt afraid and uncertain of the worth of my words. Thank you for your patience. Thank you to my editor, Madison Trammel, for believing in me and this project before I even had a proposal and inviting me to dream bigger about who it could serve. Working with you has been a joy. Thank you to Katya Covrett for initially seeing the potential in my writing. Thank you to my marketer, Nathan Kroeze, for sharing and empowering a vision for marketing as a way of serving readers and creating community. Thank you to Alexis De Weese for marketing with joy and love.

And to my dearest friends, in chapter 3 I wrote that "I am one who hopes because I am one who has been shaped by the hope of others, whose hurts are held in the hearts of others, and whose faith when fragile is augmented by the faith of those who are strong." In those words, I most meant you. Carol Collier, my soul sister, your friendship is glistening grace; like dew, your presence so frequently refreshes my soul. Scott Collier, your courageous trust in Jesus while walking toward death was one of the most beautiful things I ever had the privilege of seeing. Scott and Carol, my only regret in writing this book is that I could not find a place fitting enough for your beautiful story. I'll never forget sitting in your home this past February as the four of us shared the wonder of the joy of Jesus that comes in sorrow. In those moments, heaven touched earth. To Sarah Ocando, thank you for embodying the love that welcomes weakness. To Mish Moore, I hope you're happy with how "our" book turned out. Your courage amazes me. Josh and Rachel Allen, you have been Christ to me and Ryan, standing with us in sorrow and welcoming us into your home. To Katie Casselberry and my other college roommates and suitemates from the beginning years of my illness, Jess Jeremiah, Olivia Pelts, Mish, Becca Elder, Emily Parke, and Rachel Cheng, you each taught me how to receive love in weakness, and without you I'm not sure I would have known how to let the community of faith support me all these years. There are so many other friends whose practical presence has given me and Ryan faith when our hope was nearly dry—small groups at church, college friends, friends through our time at Denver Seminary. For all of you, we are thankful.

To Ryan, my love, you are more like Jesus than you know. You said yes to a lifetime of suffering when you made your vows to me. And you say yes, again and again, with every cup of coffee you hand me on each slow morning, every grace you give in overlooking my irritability, the steadiness you offer in the middle of my storminess, and your fearless willingness to walk with me into every dark corner of suffering and shame. I better know and trust Jesus because I see his face in yours every single day.

And Jesus, this book is my small offering of gratitude for the grace of your life. To dwell with you in sorrow and joy is a gift, and I can't wait to see your face. Your kingdom is what lasts.

K.J. Ramsey (BA, Covenant College; MA, Denver Seminary) is a licensed professional counselor, writer, and recovering idealist who believes sorrow and joy coexist. Her writing has been published in *Christianity Today, Relevant, The Huffington Post, Fathom Magazine, Health Central,* and others on the integration of theology, psychology, and spiritual formation. She and her husband live in Denver, Colorado. Follow K.J.'s writing at **kjramsey.com** and across social media (with special love for Instagram) at **@kjramseywrites**.

May you have courage to pay attention to your body, your relationships, and this moment as places where God is already present.

Seek to live in the courage of repentance by receiving Embodied, K.J.'s ongoing letter for living at the intersection of sorrow and joy. Sign up at **kjramsey.com/embodied**. And make space to talk about the hard things in your life in more than hushed tones by tuning in to This Too Shall Last, the podcast: **kjramsey.com/podcast**.